For Kimberly and Ellie

Acknowledgments

As I get to the end of a book project, I become more like a hermit in a cave, singularly focused on getting everything done on a tight schedule. But books can't happen in isolation, and I was fortunate enough to have these wonderful people just outside the cave entrance, waiting with positive words and, on occasion, dessert.

This book (as well as all the others) exists because of the wonderful patience and encouragement from my wife, Kimberly, and my daughter, Ellie.

My editor Cliff Colby has shepherded the project from the beginning, while Scout Festa, Danielle Foster, and Valerie Haynes Perry put their amazing talents to work to create a high-quality finished product.

Several people at Apple have helped with answers to my questions over several revisions of this book, including Janette Barrios, Keri Walker, Monica Sarkar, Lacey Haines, and Simon Pope.

Glenn Fleishman, Agen Schmitz, and Andrew Laurence continue to be the best virtual officemates, sounding boards, and friends a guy could have.

About Jeff Carlson

Author and photographer Jeff Carlson is a columnist for the *Seattle Times*, a senior editor at *TidBITS* (tidbits.com), and a writer for publications such as *Macworld* and *Photographic Elements Techniques*. He is the author of *The iPad for Photographers, Second Edition*; *The OS X Mavericks Pocket Guide*; and *Take Control of Your Digital Photos on the Mac*, among many other books. He believes there's never enough coffee, and does his best to test that theory. Find more information about him at jeffcarlson.com, and follow him on Twitter at @jeffcarlson.

Contents

Introduction xv
Conventions Used in This Book xvii
    Referring to iPad models xvii
    Popovers xviii
    Navigating settings xviii
    The Share menu xix

Chapter 1: Meet the iPad Air and the iPad mini 1
Power On and Set Up the iPad 2
iPad Essentials 4
    Sleep and wake 5
    Sleep and wake using a Smart Cover 5
    Power off 5
    Home screen 6
    Launch and run apps 7
    Switch quickly between apps 7
    Change screen orientation 9
    Lock screen rotation 10
    Adjust screen brightness 11
    Charge the iPad battery 12
    Conserve battery life 13
    What if the battery dies? 13
Multi-Touch Gestures 14
    Tap 14
    Touch and hold 14
    Drag 14
    Flick and swipe 15
    Pinch 15

Rotate 15
Shake 15
Use two hands 16
Work with Text 16
Type text 16
Split or move the keyboard *18*
Use alternate keyboards *19*
Auto-Correction *20*
Shortcuts *20*
Select text 21
Cut, Copy, Paste, and Replace 22
Voice dictation 23
Ask Siri for Assistance 24
Sync with a Computer 26
Disconnect the iPad 28
Set up Wi-Fi sync 28
Special sync options 28
Update the system software 30
Connect to the Internet Using Wi-Fi 30
Choose a Wi-Fi access point 31
Connect to a Wi-Fi network manually 32
Disconnect from a Wi-Fi network 33
Turn off Wi-Fi 34
Connect to the Internet Using Cellular Data 35
Understand cellular service 36
Activate cellular service 37
Measure your cellular data usage 38
Choose which apps can use cellular data 38
Add or cancel cellular service 38
Share the Internet connection using Personal Hotspot 39
Use iCloud 40
Set up iCloud 40
Sync data to iCloud 41
iCloud backup 42
Use Notification Center 42
Activate Do Not Disturb 44

Use Control Center 46
Connect to Bluetooth Devices. 46
   Pair the iPad and the device 47
   Forget the Bluetooth device. 48
Mirror Video 48
Print Using AirPrint. 49
Search Using Spotlight. 51

Chapter 2: Get and Use Apps 53
Find and Install Apps 54
   The App Store on the iPad 54
   The App Store within iTunes on a computer 57
   Automatically install purchased apps. 57
   Run iPhone apps on the iPad 57
Update Apps 58
Remove Apps 59
   On the iPad 59
   In iTunes. 60
Share Apps 61
Set App Preferences 62
Customize the Home Screen 63
   On the iPad 63
   Organize apps into folders 64
   In iTunes. 65
   Change the Home screen image 66

Chapter 3: Browse the Web. 69
Access Web Sites 70
   Open and read a new Web page 70
   Reload or cancel. 71
   Read uncluttered pages using Reader 72
   View your browsing history 73
   Open new pages 73
   Access pages on other devices using iCloud Tabs. 74
   View links using Shared Links. 75

Watch videos 75
Close pages 76
Search the Web **77**
Search within a Web page *77*
Read Pages Later with Reading List **79**
Create and Organize Bookmarks **80**
Open a bookmarked page 80
Create a new bookmark 80
Edit a bookmark 81
Add a Web page to the Home screen 82
Share a page via AirDrop 83
Share a page's address via email 84
Share a page via Twitter or Facebook 84
AutoFill Forms **86**
Enable AutoFill 86
Store a new login 87
iCloud Keychain 88
AutoFill contact information 89
Maintain Web Privacy **89**
Private browsing 89
Privacy settings 90

Chapter 4: Communicate Using Mail and Messages **91**
Set Up Mail **92**
Sync mail accounts from a computer 92
Set up an account on the iPad 92
Read Mail Messages **94**
Check for new mail 96
Check mail manually *96*
Get new mail using Push *97*
Check mail on a schedule *97*
Read email conversations 98
Navigate accounts and mailboxes 99
View file attachments 100
Act on special data 101
View information about senders and recipients 102

. . . . 132
. . . . 132
. . . . 134
. . . . 135
. . . . 136
. . . . 138
. . . . 139
. . . . 140
. . . . 141
to Stream *143*
ared Photo Stream *143*
d Photo Stream *143*
. . . . **144**
. . . . **145**
tos **145**
. . . . 146
. . . . 146
ontact 146
paper 146
V or projector **147**
. . . . *147*
e *147*
hotos and videos back to the computer 148

Books and Magazines **149**
App 150
he iBooks Store 150
n Ebooks *152*
orary *154*
lections *154*
or remove titles *155*
itles into collections *156*
es to collections *157*
or books *158*

View Photos
View a photo
View photos in locations
View photos in albums
Add photos to albums
Edit photos
Play a video
Use iCloud Photo Stream
Share a Photo Stream
Add photos to a Shared Pho
Like and comment on a Sh
Add subscribers to a Shar
View a Slideshow
Share Photos
Share one or more pho
Print a photo
Copy a photo
Assign a photo to a c
Use a photo as wall
View photos on a T
Using AirPlay
Using a video cab
Sync imported p

Chapter 7: Read
Install the iBooks
Get Books from t
Import Your Ow
Browse Your Li
Manage co
Rearrange
Organize
Move titl
Search f

Cha
Shoot
Cap
Choos
Zoom i
Capture Vid
Make FaceTin
Set up your
Set up a Face'
Make a FaceTin
View recent calls
Add a contact to th

Chapter 6: View Phot
Getting Photos onto the iF
Sync photos from the con
Sync with photo manageme
Sync with a folder
Import photos from a camera
Import photos from email
Import photos from other apps

Read Books and PDFs 158
    Navigate a book 159
    Navigate an illustrated book 160
    Navigate a PDF 161
Search Text 162
Change Appearance 164
    Adjust screen brightness 164
    Change theme 164
    Enable Scrolling View 164
    Change text size and font 165
Use Bookmarks, Highlights, and Notes 166
    Create a new bookmark 166
    Create a new highlight 166
    Change highlight coloring 167
    Create a new note 167
    Return to a bookmark, highlight, or note 168
    Share a passage 169
Look Up Word Definitions 169
Other Ebook Readers 170
Read Magazines with Newsstand 172

Chapter 8: Entertain Yourself 173
Sync Media 174
    Choose which media to sync 174
    Create a Smart Playlist in iTunes 176
Sync Media Using iTunes Match 177
    Download iTunes Match tracks 178
    Upgrade low-quality songs 179
Play Music 179
    Navigate songs 181
    Shuffle songs 182
    Repeat playback 182
    Play iTunes Radio 182
    Play Genius Mixes 183
    Listen to audiobooks 184

Create Music Playlists...184
 Build a playlist...184
 Create a Genius playlist...185
Play Videos...186
 Video sync options..186
 Watch a movie...187
Buy or Rent a Video...189
 Download or stream previously purchased videos..............190
Watch Your Own Movies..190
 Convert DVDs..191
Stream Media Between Devices...191
 AirPlay...191
 Home Sharing..192
 Set up Home Sharing...193
 Play media stored on another machine...........................193
 Streaming-video services..194

Chapter 9: Find Yourself with Maps............................195
Find Yourself...196
 Map views...198
Find Locations..199
 Get information about a location..................................200
 Drop a pin..201
Get Directions..202
 Follow the directions...204
Find Your Friends...205
 Add a friend..206
 Find friends temporarily..206
 Be notified when a friend is near (or leaving)....................206

Chapter 10: Be Productive.....................................207
Sync Personal Information...208
 iCloud, Google, or Yahoo wireless sync............................208
 Exchange sync...209
 iTunes sync...209

Manage Your Schedule 210
    View your calendar 210
    Create or edit an event 212
    Reply to an event invitation 214
    Hide, show, or edit calendars 215
    Share iCloud calendars 215
Manage Your Contacts 216
    Find a contact 217
    Create or edit a contact 219
    Share a contact 220
    Receive a shared contact 221
    Import Facebook or Twitter contacts 222
    Link contacts 222
    Delete a contact 223
Take Notes 223
    Create a note 223
    Edit a note 224
    Delete a note 225
    Sync notes 225
    Share notes 225
Set Up Reminders 226
Move Data Files to and from the iPad 228
    Sync with iCloud or network services 228
    Use email 229
    Use AirDrop 229
    Copy to the Apps pane 230

Chapter 11: Be Secure 231
Set a Passcode to Unlock 232
iCloud Keychain 234
Use a VPN 235
Set Up Usage Restrictions 236
Use Find My iPad 238
    Set up Find My iPad 238
    Take action on a lost iPad 239

Encrypt iPad Backup 241
Control Access to Your Data. 241
      Limit ad tracking. 242

Chapter 12: Troubleshooting 243
Restart the iPad 244
When an App Crashes 244
If an App Is Sluggish or Unresponsive 244
Reinstall an App 246
Connectivity Issues 248
If the iPad Doesn't Appear in iTunes 249
Battery Issues 250
Reset the iPad 250
Restore the iPad to Factory Defaults 251
Force the iPad into Recovery Mode 252

Index 253

Introduction

The original iPad's debut seemed like a grand experiment. It was an impressive new device, but would people actually buy it? Microsoft had sold PC/tablet hybrids for years without much traction. But when customers did buy the iPad—in massive, unexpected numbers—I honestly had a hard time figuring out why. Don't get me wrong—I love the iPad and use it every day, but I'm also a nerd who writes about technology for a living. I wondered why Apple has sold more than 100 million iPads to date. And then I realized the secret to the iPad's ongoing success.

The iPad is the first real spontaneous device. It's not as bulky as a laptop, and it doesn't need to be anchored in one room of the house the way a desktop computer usually is. The iPad can be anywhere in the house, or with you on the bus or train, and is a godsend for anyone who frequently travels by air in cramped middle seats. You can pick it up and search for something—like an actor's name while watching TV—without having to relocate to "the computer" or trying to remember to look up the detail later. Heck, if you also own an Apple TV, you can play a video stored on the iPad directly on your high-definition television. You can take the iPad into the kitchen and use an app such as Epicurious to find a recipe and cook a meal.

At the same time, the iPad—even the iPad mini— is not ultra compact like the iPhone. Although the iPad and iPhone share many features, the iPad's larger screen does make a difference when interacting with software, viewing photos, and reading electronic books (especially if you increase the text size because your eyes don't see as well as they used to).

So what is the iPad? It's all the things I mentioned, enhanced by the way you interact with it—by touch. It's the first gadget in a long, long time that really makes a huge difference to use in person rather than just read about online. The iPad mini is thin and light, which makes a difference every time you pick it up—and, being a tablet, it's almost always in your hands when you use it. The iPad Air is also slim and lighter than its predecessors. Both models offer incredible high-resolution Retina screens and fast processors for the best performance on a tablet. You forget you're using a computer and focus on making music, watching an HD movie, reading a book, playing a game, creating a presentation, or video-chatting with remote friends and family members.

Also, this is just the beginning: Apple believes the iPad is the future of computing. The iPad is no longer tethered to a computer and can operate on its own. Data can be backed up using Apple's free iCloud service. Or, if you choose to continue to sync with a Mac or Windows PC, you can do so over a Wi-Fi network instead of using the iPad's sync cable. As someone who uses the iPad many times a day, every day, I'm inclined to agree that this is definitely a "post-PC" device.

Conventions Used in This Book

The iPad is a computer, but it introduces a few new ways of interacting with software that differ from conventions used on computers running OS X or Microsoft Windows. Here's how I refer to a few things that crop up throughout the book.

Referring to iPad models

This book focuses on the iPad Air and the iPad mini with Retina screen (**Figure 1**), but the information applies just as well to the iPad 2 and original iPad mini, which Apple still sells, and to the third- and fourth-generation full-size iPads.

When I refer to an "iPad," in nearly all cases I'm talking about any of those models, since they all run iOS 7. The original iPad from 2010 can't run Apple's latest operating system version, so I recommend you seek out the third edition of this book if that's the model you own. Occasionally I'll mention specific models where appropriate.

Figure 1
*iPad Air and
iPad mini with
Retina display*

Popovers

It's taken me a while to not think of breakfast pastry when I type this, but a "popover" (Apple's term) is a relatively new interface element introduced on the iPad. A popover is a floating list of options that appears when you tap some buttons (**Figure 2**).

Figure 2
A popover in Safari

Navigating settings

When I mention a system preference in the Settings app, I do so with symbols to indicate the hierarchy of taps. So, when I write *Settings > Safari > Passwords & AutoFill*, that translates to:

1. At the Home screen, tap the Settings app.

2. Tap the Safari button in the left-hand pane.

3. Tap the Passwords & AutoFill button in the right-hand pane (**Figure 3**).

Figure 3
Navigating settings

The Share menu

This important interface element shows up in nearly every app. The Share menu (⬆) focuses on sharing, but many apps also include non-sharing commands in the menu. In nearly every case, when you tap this control you're accessing commands that perform some sort of action, such as sharing, printing, copying, and the like (**Figure 3**).

Figure 3
The Share menu in the Photos app

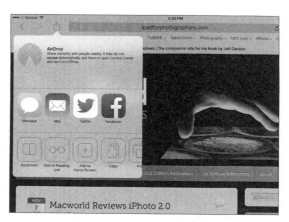

1

Meet the iPad Air and the iPad mini

It's not often that something really new appears. Desktop and laptop computers are so commonplace, it's hard to believe that not too long ago you could go to the airport and see maybe one or two personal computers, total. The iPhone represented a new direction for Apple—and, it turns out, the cell phone industry—but it was still just a smartphone executed really well. (What's interesting is that the iPad actually came first: Apple took the work it put into developing a tablet operating system and decided to bring it to market first as a phone.)

Companies—Apple included—had tried to create tablet computers for years and failed. So what makes the iPad different? The iPad isn't the same old desktop software pressed into a laptop case that's missing a keyboard. It was designed from scratch to be a mobile tablet. And as you'll see when you use it and as you read this book, that's a profound difference. It's not a laptop replacement (although it takes that role for some people), and it's not a limited handheld device, either. The iPad shares the same underlying operating system as the iPhone, so many aspects may be familiar if you already own an iPhone or iPod touch, but it doesn't rely on old computing crutches like using a mouse pointer or forcing the user to wrangle a sprawling file system.

Instead, the iPad is a big step forward based on an old, simple idea: Anyone can take advantage of computing and digital media, without needing to be a computer expert—or even a "computer person." People shouldn't have to understand a hierarchical file system or virtual memory. This idea sounds simple, yet it's extremely difficult to do. Even after years of making computers "for the rest of us," Apple is very close to doing it.

The iPad is the first step toward a new future. I'm not talking about robots and jet packs—though you might think I sound like I've spent too much time at a high altitude—but rather a dramatic break from what we expect computers to be. And that's a truly new idea.

Power On and Set Up the iPad

An iPad doesn't require a computer at all—though one is definitely helpful to have. Apple's step-by-step getting started process is simple, but you're prompted to make several decisions about how your data is synchronized and where it will live. (These steps vary a bit depending on how you're syncing your data and whether you're upgrading from a previous device. For example, if you begin connected to a computer, you select a Wi-Fi network after selecting an existing device profile.) But the process is easy to follow, so don't worry if these steps don't match your experience exactly. If you've already done this stage, skip ahead to "iPad Essentials."

1. To power the iPad on for the first time, press and briefly hold the button at the top of the iPad until the Apple logo appears.

2. Slide the "Slide to set up" slider to get started.

3. Choose your language and region.

4. Tap the name of a nearby Wi-Fi network and enter its password to get online. Tap Join.

5. On the Location Services screen, tap Enable Location Services. This option allows apps such as Maps to use data related to your whereabouts. You can choose to disable Location Services if you're concerned about privacy, but that limits the functionality of many things, such as Find My iPad. (You can enable or disable the option later in the iPad's settings, too.)

6. Choose whether to set up the device as a new iPad or to restore data from an iCloud or iTunes backup, and then tap Next.

   ■ To set up a new iPad, you'll need to enter an Apple ID (or create a new one if you don't have one). The Apple ID is what you normally use to buy media from iTunes, the App Store, or the Mac App Store.

   ■ For iCloud, you'll need to enter your iCloud user name and password. Then, choose the latest saved backup and tap Restore. After the data is restored, see step 7 and then you're done.

   ■ For iTunes, you'll need to connect a sync cable between the iPad and the computer running iTunes. In iTunes, choose the name of the device you want to use as the backup source. The iPad will restart, and iTunes will sync the settings and content from the backup to it. You will then need to repeat some of the setup steps.

7. Review the Terms and Conditions for using the iPad, and agree to them by tapping the Agree button.

8. Create a four-digit passcode. It's not required, but I highly encourage you to use a passcode.

9. If you want to use Siri, tap Use Siri.

10. If you want Apple to receive anonymized usage data and diagnostic information in the event something crashes, tap the Automatically Send button in the Diagnostics screen. If you'd prefer not to share the data, tap Don't Send.

11. Lastly, tap the Start Using iPad button to finish setup.

tip If you already have a lot of apps for your iPhone or iPod touch, iTunes may want to transfer them all to the iPad. Instead of deselecting unwanted apps one by one, do this: In the Apps tab in iTunes, Command-click (Mac) or Control-click (Windows) one app's checkbox to deselect them all. Click Apply to make the change. Then, go through the list and enable the apps you want to transfer.

note I own an iPhone, which goes with me everywhere. Because my iPad acts as an extension of all of my important data, I chose to use the data from my iPhone the first time I set up an iPad instead of configuring it from scratch. If you take this route, you'll still need to do some cleanup work; I found that some universal iPad apps (ones which can run on either an iPhone or the iPad) did not transfer automatically, but otherwise the process was smooth.

iPad Essentials

After the iPad is set up, and each time you press the power button or Home button, a Slide to Unlock control appears. Drag your finger left to right along the slider to advance past the opening screen.

Sleep and wake

Once powered on, the iPad rarely needs to be turned off. Instead, when you're finished using it, press the power button once (without holding it) to put it into a low-powered sleep mode.

> **note** The iPad automatically goes to sleep after 5 minutes of inactivity to conserve battery power. You can change that amount in the Settings app by tapping General, then Auto-Lock, and tapping a time duration (2, 5, 10, or 15 minutes, or Never if you want to always put the iPad to sleep manually).

To wake the iPad, press the power button or the Home button and then use the Slide to Unlock control.

Sleep and wake using a Smart Cover

Apple's Smart Covers were designed alongside the iPad: They interact with magnets built into the iPad's case to align the cover and also provide a nifty sleep/wake feature. Open the Smart Cover to wake the iPad, or close the cover to put the iPad to sleep. (Other companies also make cases that interact with the magnets in the same way.)

You can disable this behavior by going to Settings > General and then turning off the iPad Cover Lock/Unlock option.

Power off

It's rare that I turn off the iPad completely—usually only when something seems to be wrong and I want to restart it, or if I know I won't be using it for an extended period of time (like *that's* realistic). To do so, press and hold the power button until the red Slide to Power Off control appears. Slide it to turn off the power.

tip   To prevent just anyone from unlocking your iPad and accessing your data, I highly recommend that you specify a passcode that must be entered first. See Chapter 11 for more information.

Home screen

After you've unlocked the iPad, you're taken to the Home screen, which displays the software applications (or "apps") stored on the device (**Figure 1.1**).

Figure 1.1
Apps on the Home screen

When your iPad holds more than 20 apps, a new Home screen is created; you can see how many screens are available by looking at the dots near the bottom of the screen. Swipe left or right to switch between each screen. The shelf at the bottom of the screen holds up to six apps that remain visible on every Home screen.

 Yes, that's right. Although the shelf holds four apps initially, you can add two more apps of your choosing.

Press the Home button in the bezel at any time to exit an app and go to the last Home screen you were viewing. If you press the button when you're already on a Home screen, you're taken to the first screen.

Launch and run apps

Tap once on an app's icon to launch it. (That's it. No double-clicking, pressing Command-O, or hitting Return and wondering if Windows is actually opening the program.)

Unlike most desktop or laptop computers, the iPad displays one app at a time, which takes over the entire screen; it's not possible, for example, to have Mail on one side of the screen and Safari on the other. To switch to a different app, press the Home button and then tap the other app's icon from the Home screen.

 For more information about customizing the Home screen and working with apps, see Chapter 2.

Switch quickly between apps

Even though only one app is visible at a time, the iPad runs several apps at the same time (a feature known as *multitasking*). When you exit one app, it's effectively frozen until you return to it. Some apps can continue to work in the background—Mail can send and receive messages, Music can play music, and so forth—but most apps wait until they're activated, at which point they resume where they left off.

- To view your most recent apps, press the Home button twice quickly. (You can also swipe up with four or five fingers, a setting located at Settings > General > Multitasking Gestures.) The multitasking interface appears, revealing current and recent apps (**Figure 1.2**). Flick sideways on the list to view more apps, and tap the app you wish to open.

- When you're viewing an app, swipe left or right with four or five fingers to switch to the next or previous app, bypassing a trip to the Home screen.

- Pinch with five fingers to return to the Home screen without pressing the physical Home button.

Figure 1.2
The multitasking interface

tip   iOS tries to convey the idea of depth by zooming in when you launch an app, zooming out when you return to the home screen, and also zooming in and out of the multitasking interface. If that's too much motion for you (some people do get dizzy from it), do this: go to Settings > Accessibility >

Reduce Motion and turn the feature on. Transitions become fades instead of zooms, and the parallax effect of icons (where the background shifts slightly depending on the iPad's movement) is disabled.

Change screen orientation

One of the coolest features of the iPad is the accelerometer, a sensor inside that knows how the iPad is being held, including whether the screen is in a tall (portrait) or wide (landscape) orientation. Knowing the position is important, because the iPad's operating system adjusts to the orientation: Hold the iPhoto app in portrait position and the image thumbnails appear at the bottom of the screen; rotate the display to the landscape position and the thumbnails appear to the left (**Figure 1.3**).

Figure 1.3
Screen rotation

Landscape
orientation

Portrait orientation

Simply turn the iPad to change its orientation. In fact, from the software's point of view, there is no "correct" orientation. No matter how you hold it, the screen contents rotate to be right-side up.

Screen orientation is just a parlor trick for the accelerometer, however. Because it calculates the iPad's position in three dimensions, it also knows at what angle you're holding the device and responds to that. Plus, a built-in gyroscope and compass make it possible for the iPad to calculate where it's being held in physical space. Many games take advantage of these features, turning the entire iPad into the game controller to affect what's happening onscreen.

Lock screen rotation

You may not want the screen to adjust its orientation at times, like when you're reading while lying down. The iPad offers two ways to do this: The iPad side switch, located next to the volume adjustment button, can be set to lock the orientation or to mute audio; or, you can tap a button in Control Center.

tip When the side switch is configured to lock screen orientation, you can still easily mute the iPad's audio: Press and hold the volume-down button for a couple of seconds. The volume level dips and then drops to zero.

To choose which behavior to use, you need to specify how the iPad side switch is used:

1. Open the Settings app and tap General.

2. Under the "Use Side Switch to" heading, tap to choose either Lock Rotation or Mute.

   Based on your choice here, the *opposite* action becomes the option available in Control Center.

To lock screen orientation or mute the iPad volume using Control Center, do the following:

1. Swipe up from the bottom of the screen to reveal Control Center (**Figure 1.4**).

2. Tap the lock orientation or mute audio button, depending on the side switch setting.

Figure 1.4
Lock orientation in Control Center

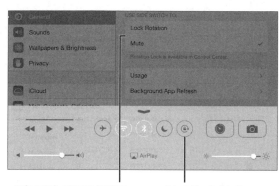

Side switch option in Settings   Orientation Lock button

Adjust screen brightness

Normally, the iPad's ambient-light sensor adjusts the screen brightness automatically according to its surroundings. If you'd like to dim the light or punch it up manually, you can do so in two places:

- Go to Settings > Wallpaper & Brightness and drag the slider left (darker) or right (brighter). To always adjust manually, turn off the Auto-Brightness switch.

- Swipe up from the bottom of the screen to reveal Control Center, and adjust the brightness slider (located in the lower-right corner).

Charge the iPad battery

The iPad Air and iPad mini each include a non-removable lithium-polymer battery that provides up to 10 hours of use on a single charge. (In fact, Apple claims that 10 hours of video playback, surfing the Web using Wi-Fi, or listening to music are possible.) You can check the state of the battery by looking at the indicator in the upper-right corner of the screen (**Figure 1.5**).

Figure 1.5
Battery indicator

Current battery charge

 To show or hide the percentage next to the battery indicatory, go to Settings > General > Usage and tap the Battery Percentage switch.

Actual battery life depends on how you use the iPad, of course—playing a video game that makes extensive use of 3D graphics is more demanding on the processor and will eat up power faster than reading a book in iBooks. As the battery nears depletion, warning messages appear when 20 percent and 10 percent of the power remains. After that, the iPad becomes unresponsive and needs to be charged to function again.

To replenish the battery's charge, plug the iPad's sync cable into the included power adapter. You can also plug the sync cable into your computer to sync and recharge, but there's a catch: Your computer's USB port may not have the oomph to do it. If that's the case, you'll see "Not Charging" in the power indicator at the upper-right corner of the screen.

The specifications for running power over USB call for at least 5V (volts), but the iPad requires more than that. Some computers, such as recent Apple laptops and desktops, can optionally provide as much as 12V when a device that requires it is connected. In that case, the iPad will charge, but more slowly than when connected to the power adapter. The upside is that when the iPad is connected to a low-power USB port, the battery does not deplete; in fact, it will trickle-charge slowly when the iPad is asleep, and keep a steady level when it's awake.

Conserve battery life

You can take steps to make the most of the battery's charge. No need to be slavish about these, but you'll definitely want to implement them when you get a low battery notice:

- Turn down the screen brightness.

- Turn off Wi-Fi if you're not within range of a wireless network.

- Turn off Bluetooth if you're not using it.

- Disable notifications.

- Disable cellular networking (provided you own a cellular model) if you're not accessing data online (discussed later in this chapter).

What if the battery dies?

Batteries lose capacity over time, but sometimes a battery won't hold a charge for nearly as long as it once did. If the iPad is still under warranty (one year, or two years if you also purchased AppleCare for it), contact Apple and ask for a replacement iPad. If an Apple retail store is nearby, an Apple Genius will be able to diagnose whether the battery is faulty.

If you're out of warranty and the iPad "requires service due to the battery's diminished ability to hold an electrical charge" (in Apple's words), then you can take advantage of Apple's battery replacement service. For $99, Apple will replace the entire iPad (so be sure you've synchronized it before sending it off). See www.apple.com/support/ipad/service/battery/ for more information.

Multi-Touch Gestures

You probably noticed that when you opened the iPad's box, no stylus fell out. Until fairly recently, most tablet computers and handhelds required that you use a plastic pencil to do anything. The iPad, instead, is designed for your fingers. You interact with the software on the screen by touching, tapping, swiping, and performing other Multi-Touch gestures. Many controls are intuitive: Tap the Edit button in Contacts, for example, to edit a person's information. Other motions may not be obvious at first, but they quickly become natural.

Tap

As you've no doubt discovered, the most obvious action is to point at an area of the screen, like a button or other control, and lightly tap with one finger. Sometimes, you'll want to double-tap the screen, such as when you want to zoom in on a section of a Web page in Safari.

 When you encounter an On/Off switch, you can slide the switch if you want, or simply tap it to change its state.

Touch and hold

Instead of quickly tapping and lifting your finger from the screen, there are times when you want to touch the screen and maintain contact to elicit an action (for example, see "Work with Text," ahead).

Drag

Touch and hold a point on the screen, then move your finger across the glass. Drag a Web page in Safari from bottom to top to scroll as you read.

 Don't worry if a finger touchs a screen edge when you're holding the iPad Air or iPad mini; the software automatically ignores that contact.

Flick and swipe

A flick (yes, that's Apple's official name for it) is like a drag, but faster. On a Web page, touch the screen and flick your finger to "throw" the page in any direction. The software simulates the physics of the motion and slows the scrolling page until it comes to a stop, based on the velocity of the flick.

A swipe is similar to a flick, but you drag something (usually horizontally) a bit more slowly. You swipe a photo from right to left to advance to the next picture, for instance.

 The iPad's screen responds to the electricity in your fingers, not to pressure. Pressing harder on the display doesn't improve its response.

Pinch

When you want to zoom in or out on an item, such as a map, a photo, or a Web page, touch two fingers to the screen and pinch them together (to zoom out) or spread them apart (to zoom in).

Rotate

Press two fingers to the screen and rotate them in a circle to rotate something, such as a photo in the Photos app.

Shake

Yes, that's right, give the iPad a good shake. The accelerometer recognizes the motion as an intentional vibration, and software that's been written to handle the gesture can act on it. For example, when you're typing in the Notes app and make a mistake, shake the iPad to bring up a dialog that gives you the option to undo the last action. I've found that shaking front to back, not side to side, seems to be more responsive.

Use two hands

The iPad's entire screen is filled with sensors, so take advantage of the large display area and use both hands. One obvious application is the keyboard that appears when you're entering text; since it's nearly full size, you can type as you would on a physical keyboard.

For another example, look to Apple's Keynote app: Touch and hold a slide with the finger of one hand, and then use your other hand to tap other slides to select them all in a group. Numerous games and other apps also accept two-handed input.

Work with Text

It's one thing to view photos and movies, but how do you enter and edit text? Whether you're typing a Web address, adding an event to your calendar, or composing a letter, you need to know how to put letters to screen. You'll encounter the following basic operations throughout the iPad environment.

Type text

Whenever you tap an editable text area, the iPad's software keyboard slides up from the bottom of the screen (**Figure 1.6**). Type on it as you would a regular keyboard, keeping a few things in mind:

- The screen can't accommodate a full-sized keyboard, so some characters appear where you may not expect them. For example, you type an exclamation point (!) by holding the Shift (⬆) key and tapping the comma (,) key. Number keys are accessed by tapping the ".?123" key, and symbols such as the equals sign (=) are available after next tapping the "#+=" key.

Figure 1.6
The onscreen keyboard

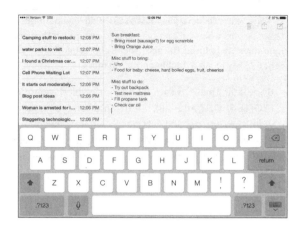

- The keyboard can vary depending on the context of the text field. When you're in the Address field in Safari, the Return key reads "Go." At other times, you may not see letters at all, such as when a number keypad and options for different functions appear when you edit values in Numbers.

> **tip** To quickly enter other domain name suffixes, like .net or .org, touch and hold the period (.) key. A pop-up menu presents other options for you to tap to add to the text. The same is true for typing accented characters.

- To hide the keyboard without exiting the text field, tap the ⌨ key.

- You can end a sentence with a period by simply tapping two spaces after a word. (This shortcut came about on the iPhone, where the period key doesn't appear on the first screen of keys.) If you'd rather turn off this feature, go to Settings > General > Keyboard and disable the "." Shortcut option.

tip   Want to know the most useful iPad keyboard tip? To type an apostrophe, which isn't on the main screen, touch the comma (,) key and slide your finger up to insert the apostrophe character. You can do the same with the period (.) key to get a double-quotation mark.

- By default, the Caps Lock feature is disabled (nobody likes it when PEOPLE SHOUT, after all), but if you often type acronyms or otherwise want the option, go to Settings > General > Keyboard and turn on the Enable Caps Lock option. When typing, quickly double-tap the Shift key to enter Caps Lock mode; the face of the key is highlighted (versus just the up-arrow icon when normal Shift is active).

Split or move the keyboard

When you're holding the iPad, versus resting it on a flat surface, how do you type? Balanced on one hand and typing with the other hand? With your thumbs, like on a smartphone? I fall in the latter camp. The narrower width of the iPad Air compared to earlier full-size iPads makes it more comfortable to type this way (and the iPad mini is just the right size for thumb-typing). But everyone has different hand sizes.

To make it easier for people to type, Apple offers a split-keyboard option. The keys can also be repositioned vertically on the screen.

1. In an app that accepts text input, tap to place the cursor and bring up the onscreen keyboard.

2. Drag the right edge of the ⌨ key up the screen; as you drag, the keyboard splits (**Figure 1.7**).

3. To position the split keyboard higher on the screen, continue dragging up.

To return the keyboard back to its original, joined state, drag the ⌨ key back to the bottom of the screen. You can also touch and hold the key and choose to merge the keyboard halves while keeping their vertical position.

Figure 1.7
*The split
keyboard*

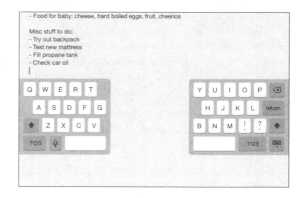

Use alternate keyboards

A virtual keyboard can take any shape, which also means it can assume
nearly any language, including non-Roman ones such as Chinese or even
playful Emoji characters.

1. Go to Settings > General > Keyboard and tap the Keyboards button.

2. Tap the Add New Keyboard button.

3. Choose an alternate keyboard, then return to the previous screen.

To switch between keyboards while you're typing, tap the 🌐 key that
now appears. Or, touch and hold the key to select from a pop-up list of
active keyboards (**Figure 1.8**).

Figure 1.8
*Alternate
keyboards*

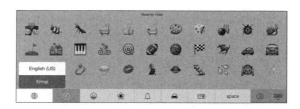

Auto-Correction

This extremely helpful feature debuted on the iPhone, where the smaller screen size makes it more challenging to hit the right keys as you're typing. As you type, the iPad analyzes your letters to look for patterns and offers suggestions in a little pop-up box (**Figure 1.9**). To accept the suggestion, type a space or punctuation. To ignore it, either tap the X on the pop-up or continue typing letters. (Also see "Cut, Copy, Paste, and Replace," just ahead.)

Figure 1.9
Text auto-correction

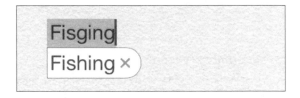

If the feature is getting in your way, go to Settings > General > Keyboard. While there, you can also disable Auto-Capitalization, which automatically enables the Shift key after you've applied punctuation.

Shortcuts

If you frequently type the same phrases, you can set up shortcuts that expand to longer items. For example, instead of writing "Cheers! Jeff" at the end of every email message, I could set up a shortcut of "cjf" to insert that text for me.

1. Go to Settings > General > Keyboard, and tap Add New Shortcut.

2. Type the text you want expanded in the Phrase field.

3. Type the shortcut text in the Shortcut field.

4. Tap the Save button.

Select text

On a computer, selecting text is easy: You position your mouse pointer, then click and drag to select the text you want. The iPad has no mouse pointer, so the process of selecting text is slightly different.

1. Within any range of text (not just in text-entry fields), touch and hold where you want to start selecting. A magnified view of the area appears above your finger (**Figure 1.10**).

Figure 1.10
*Select text with
magnification.*

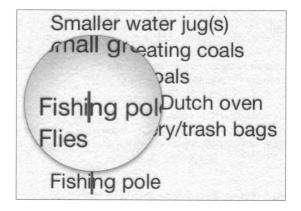

2. Position the insertion point and release your finger. As you'll see in a moment, you don't need to put the insertion point at the exact start of your selection.

3. In the pop-up that appears, choose Select to highlight the closest word; or, tap Select All to highlight a full sentence.

4. Drag the handles to the left and right of the initial selection to define the full area you wish to select (**Figure 1.11**, on the next page). If you drag beyond a paragraph, the selection area broadens to include blocks of text instead of letter-by-letter selections.

Figure 1.11
Drag to highlight text.

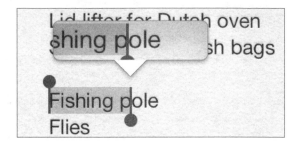

tip If you're in an editable text area (versus a read-only area like a Web page), double-tap a word to select it. Or, tap four times quickly to select an entire sentence. And here's a quick tip that doesn't apply just to editable areas: Double-tap a word, but hold the second tap to make a selection, and then drag to expand it without lifting your finger.

note Selecting text occasionally works differently depending on which app you're using. In Safari, for example, touching and holding on text on a Web page selects whichever word is under your finger; drag to select any word, lift your finger, and then expand the selection.

Cut, Copy, Paste, and Replace

When you make a selection, a set of options appears above the text.

- **Cut:** The selection is copied to memory and then removed from the content you're editing.

- **Copy:** The selected content is just copied to memory.

- **Paste:** If you've previously cut or copied some text, the Paste option appears. Tap Paste to add the content stored in memory; if a selection is made, the pasted content overwrites the selection.

- **Replace:** Does a word look misspelled? Select it and tap the Replace button. If the iPad comes up with a different spelling (or a similar word), it appears in a pop-up—tap the suggestion to replace the selected word (**Figure 1.12**).

Figure 1.12
Selection options

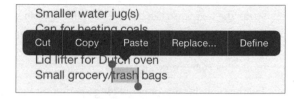

After choosing
the Replace option

Misspelled words also appear with a dotted red underline (**Figure 1.13**). Tap once on the word to view suggestions.

Figure 1.13
*A misspelled
word underlined*

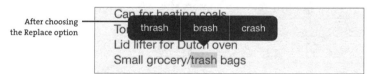

tip Selecting, copying, and pasting aren't reserved solely for text. In Safari, for example, you can select a range of text that also includes an image, copy it, and then open Mail and paste the formatted content into an outgoing message.

Voice dictation

If you're more comfortable speaking instead of typing on the iPad's keyboard, definitely give voice dictation a try; I'm regularly amazed at the quality of the transcription.

1. Tap any text field to make the onscreen keyboard appear.

2. Tap the Voice Dictation ( ) key.

3. Speak the text you'd like to type. Remember to speak punctuation, like "period" or "question mark," to include it. For example, to type *Robert, did you remember to buy groceries?*, you'd say, "Robert comma did you remember to buy groceries question mark."

4. Tap the Done button, or pause long enough for the iPad to guess that you're finished. Your text appears after a few seconds.

Ask Siri for Assistance

In the past, if I was talking to a computer, I was probably saying things that shouldn't be repeated in respectable company. With Siri on the iPad, not only has my language cleaned up, but I can get information without going to the trouble of typing a search term into Safari. The feature isn't perfect—voice recognition is difficult, science-with-a-capital-S stuff—but it works much better than you might think. It's also an evolving technology: Most of the processing occurs on Apple's massive collection of data centers, so the service improves the more people use it. (Siri works with all iPad models except the original one and the iPad 2.)

To get Siri's attention, press and hold the Home button for a couple of seconds until you see "What can I help you with?" and an active sound wave at the bottom of the screen. Then speak a question or issue a command. Siri detects when you're done talking and then acts on your query; or, if you're in a noisy environment, you can tap the button to get Siri started.

 If Siri didn't understand your question, tap the "Tap to edit" text below Siri's translation of what you said and type the correct term.

What can you ask? Really, almost anything. If Siri doesn't know the answer, it will suggest a Web search. But since Siri is designed to be an "intelligent assistant," you can also tell it to perform actions. The following are a few examples; tap the *i* button on Siri's dialog to view a list of suggested uses.

- "Is it going to rain in Sacramento tomorrow?" Siri checks the weather for that location and displays the weekly forecast.

- "Where can I find good espresso near here?" Using the iPad's Location Services feature, Siri determines where you are and then consults databases such as Yelp to find nearby businesses and provide a list. Tap a business's name to learn more about it.

- "Who won the Chelsea–Manchester United game?" Siri keeps tabs on most popular sporting events and can return current or recent scores. You could also ask when your favorite team plays next, and who their opponent will be.

- "Guide me to Glenn's house." Siri determines your current location, finds a contact matching "Glenn" (possibly requiring you to specify which Glenn you mean), and plots a route using the Maps app.

- "What's on my schedule tomorrow?" Siri retrieves your events from the Calendar app.

- "Shuffle music by the Decemberists." Play music without launching the Music app.

- "Send a text to Kim that says I'm running 10 minutes late." Siri composes a new iMessage to that person, containing the phrase you specify.

This is just a small collection of Siri's possibilities. Throughout the rest of this book, I note other instances when Siri can be helpful.

tip   If several of your contacts have the same first name, Siri asks you to choose from a list each time you mention them. To help, set up relationships in the Contacts app. For example, I opened the contact information for my father, Larry, tapped Edit, and tapped the Add Field button. In the popover that appeared, I scrolled down and tapped the Related People button. Lastly, I set the field to Child and located my contact card. Now I can say, "Send a text to my father" and Siri knows to address the message to the correct Larry.

tip   You may know Siri as a friendly woman, but the voice differs in some other countries. The voice in the United Kingdom, for instance, is male (it's almost like being helped by James Bond). Go to Settings > General > Siri > Language to choose a different language if you want. A few languages, such as English (United States) and English (Canada) offer a separate setting to choose Siri's gender.

Sync with a Computer

Although an iPad can do everything you need it to do by itself, chances are your music, movies, and other data reside on a Mac or Windows PC. A computer is also the easiest way to keep a backup of the iPad's data. iCloud backup is great, but it isn't appropriate for all situations (namely, when you don't have robust Internet connectivity).

The iPad's home base is iTunes, Apple's media hub software. If you don't have the latest version, go to www.apple.com/itunes/ to download and install it.

When you connect the iPad using the USB cable, the iPad appears in the Devices list (**Figure 1.14**). If the iPad is your only iOS device, its name is used for the button; if you sync other devices, the button is named Devices. Select your iPad to view information and options for synchronizing your data.

tip In iTunes 10 and earlier, the iPad appeared in a sidebar instead of the Devices list, as in iTunes 11. You can go back to that organization if you prefer: choose View > Show Sidebar.

Figure 1.14
The iPad in iTunes

iPad Air in
Devices list

Here's what gets transferred when you connect the iPad:

- Any new or changed data, which is added to the backup of the iPad on your computer
- New and updated apps (those downloaded on the iPad and in iTunes)
- Music, movies, and TV shows
- Podcasts
- iTunes U (university courses available via iTunes)
- Photos
- Files used by iPad apps

note You may be surprised at just how infrequently you need to sync the iPad. Using iCloud, for example, you can wirelessly sync your calendars and contacts. Application updates are also available using the included App Store app (see Chapter 2).

Disconnect the iPad

When you want to take the iPad somewhere, simply disconnect the sync cable. Unlike other USB devices, the iPad doesn't need to be ejected first.

Set up Wi-Fi sync

If you ask me, one of the best unheralded features of the iPad (and any device running iOS) is the ability to sync wirelessly. As long as your iPad is on the same Wi-Fi network as the computer to which you sync, you can leave that sync cable in a drawer or use it on a bedside table for charging. Here's how to set up Wi-Fi sync:

1. Connect the iPad to the computer using the sync cable.

2. Select the iPad in iTunes.

3. On the Summary screen, scroll down to the Options section and select "Sync with this iPad over Wi-Fi."

4. Click the Apply button.

Whenever the iPad is plugged into power and on the Wi-Fi network, a sync operation occurs. You can also initiate a manual sync from the iPad: Open Settings > General > iTunes Wi-Fi Sync, and tap the Sync Now button.

note   Even if Wi-Fi sync is enabled, the iPad will still sync when connected via the USB cable. If you're transferring a lot of data, the cable is a much faster option.

Special sync options

Synchronization mostly concerns transferring your media and related files. These options, found on the Summary screen, refine how iTunes handles the sync.

- **Open iTunes when this iPad is connected:** Select this option to launch iTunes if it's not running when you plug in the iPad.

- **Sync only checked songs and videos:** In iTunes, you can uncheck a song's checkbox to prevent it from playing (such as when you like every song on an album except one). If this option is deselected, all songs and movies are copied to the iPad, taking up more memory.

- **Prefer standard-definition videos:** Although the iPad can play Apple's HD videos, they take up much more memory. Select this option if you want to conserve storage by transferring standard-definition versions of movies.

- **Convert higher bit rate songs to [128/192/256] kbps AAC:** Selecting this option can significantly reduce the amount of space your music collection occupies by making lower- (but still decent-) quality versions of songs: 128 kbps, 192 kbps, or 256 kbps. If you've ripped your own music at higher bit rates, choose a quality level to eke out some space on the iPad.

- **Manually manage music and videos:** Wield more control over what gets transferred to the iPad. When this option is selected, you can drag songs and videos from your iTunes library to the iPad. If you decide to turn off this feature later, however, your music and videos are erased and replaced according to the options you set up in each media tab. (Personally, I don't need organization that is this granular.)

- **Configure Universal Access:** Click this button to enable options that make the iPad more usable for people with impaired vision or hearing. These controls mirror those found in Settings > General > Accessibility.

- **Encrypt local backup:** The data on the iPad is encrypted—scrambled so that if the iPad is lost or stolen, its contents can't be read. The backup stored on your computer's hard disk, however, is not encrypted. To make it inaccessible to prying eyes, activate this option, which is listed in the Backups section of the Summary screen when Automatically

Back Up is set to "This computer." A dialog appears, asking you to define and verify a password.

tip   What if you want to connect the iPad to your computer but don't want to sync? You can't change the automatic sync preference without the iPad connected. Instead, press and hold Command-Option (Mac) or Shift-Control (Windows) when you connect the iPad, and hold them until the iPad appears. It won't sync.

Update the system software

When Apple releases updates to iOS, iTunes informs you with an alert. You can also click the Check for Update button on the Summary screen to query manually. If an update is available, you're given the option of downloading and installing it.

On the iPad itself, you can check for updates by going to Settings > General > Software Update.

tip   If you say yes to the update in iTunes, you get to choose whether to download and install it right away or just download the software for later. The second option is good if you want to take advantage of a robust Internet connection (for example, you're at the office or in a coffee shop with your laptop) but plan to update the iPad at another time (when you get home).

Connect to the Internet Using Wi-Fi

Every iPad supports Wi-Fi wireless networking, enabling you to connect to the Internet using nearby access points; you may have a Wi-Fi network set up in your house or office, or you might go to a nearby "hotspot," usually a coffee shop or restaurant. A Wi-Fi network usually covers the space of a house or small building. Compare that to cellular wireless (more on that shortly), which is designed to offer miles of coverage.

Once the iPad is connected to a Wi-Fi network, you can browse the Web, send and receive email, view maps, and perform other tasks that require an Internet connection. Wi-Fi also lets you interact with other devices and computers sharing the network connection; for example, you can play a game against another iPad owner or control the music playback of a computer running iTunes.

Choose a Wi-Fi access point

When the iPad requires an Internet connection, such as for accessing email or a Web page, it checks to see if an active Wi-Fi network is within range. A dialog appears with a list of nearby networks (**Figure 1.15**). Tap the name of a network you want to join, type its password if required, and then tap the Join button on the keyboard.

Figure 1.15
Available Wi-Fi networks

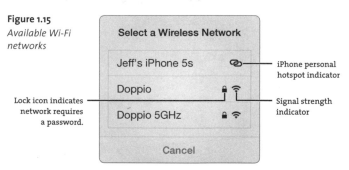

Lock icon indicates network requires a password.

iPhone personal hotspot indicator

Signal strength indicator

note Many public Wi-Fi hotspots don't require a password to join the network but do need you to log in using a Web form once you're connected. The iPad should automatically display a login form. If not, after you get onto the network, go to Safari and enter any valid Web address. The login page should appear if you need to sign in (or pay) for access.

tip If you'd rather not be interrupted by a pop-up list of networks, go to Settings > Wi-Fi and then turn off the Ask to Join Networks option.

tip Exercise good judgment when joining open, unprotected Wi-Fi networks. It's possible (and easy, for those who are savvy) to intercept the data passing between the iPad and the base station running the network. A nefarious network owner—or even someone at the next table in a coffee shop— could collect the data stream and mine it for things like passwords and credit card numbers. Unless you can vouch for the network owner, avoid paying bills or making purchases on public networks. See Chapter 11 for more information.

Connect to a Wi-Fi network manually

The iPad is helpful in displaying and connecting to available Wi-Fi networks, but there will be times when you want to link up with one manually—when you accidentally connected to the wrong network or the owner has hidden the network name for security, for instance. Here's how to connect using the Settings app (**Figure 1.16**).

Figure 1.16
Connect to Wi-Fi in Settings.

1. Go to Settings > Wi-Fi.

2. From the list that appears under Choose a Network, tap a network name.

3. If a password is required, type it into the Password field and then tap the Join button.

The network name gains a checkbox, and a Wi-Fi signal strength icon appears in the upper-left corner of the screen.

To connect to a network that isn't broadcasting its name, or if the iPad isn't listing the one you expect, do the following (**Figure 1.17**):

Figure 1.17
Join a hidden Wi-Fi network.

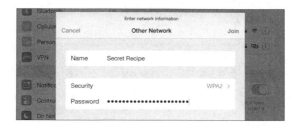

1. In the Wi-Fi screen, tap the Other button.

2. Type the network name in the Name field.

3. Tap the Security button and specify which type of encryption the network is using. If you don't know, try WPA2 first, followed by WEP (which is older and no longer secure, but still widely used).

4. Enter the network's password in the Password field that appears.

5. Tap Join to establish a connection.

> **tip** The iPad remembers Wi-Fi network names and settings, so the next time you're within range of a network you've previously joined, a connection is automatically made.

Disconnect from a Wi-Fi network

If you accidentally join the wrong network, it's easy to sever the connection. In Settings > Wi-Fi, tap the information button (ⓘ) and then tap Forget this Network.

Turn off Wi-Fi

Go to Settings > Wi-Fi and set the Wi-Fi switch to Off. Or, bring up Control Center (swipe up from the bottom of the screen) and tap the Wi-Fi button. (More on Control Center later in this chapter.) You may want to do this when conserving battery power or if you're in an area where you know a Wi-Fi network isn't available.

Use a Cellular Data Network with a Wi-Fi iPad

Instead of purchasing an iPad with Wi-Fi and cellular access (see the next page), some people are employing a different technique to provide ubiquitous Internet access.

The Novatel Wireless MiFi (www.novatelwireless.com) is a portable Wi-Fi hotspot that connects to a cellular data network. It's pocket-sized and offers the same type of always-on connection that the iPad with cellular service provides. However, it's not bound to one carrier, and it can let more than one device connect at a time.

The monthly service costs more than the iPad's cellular setup, but you're not tied to Apple's preferred carriers. If you need to connect several devices over Wi-Fi (like the iPad, an iPhone, and a laptop) or can't get good reception using your cellular provider, something like the MiFi may be perfect.

If you already own an iPhone 4 or later, another option is available. For a monthly fee to your cellular service provider, you can set up the iPhone as a portable hotspot, connecting up to five devices via Wi-Fi.

Connect to the Internet Using Cellular Data

For people who tend to travel often or who need more frequent access to the Internet than is afforded by Wi-Fi hotspots, Apple offers iPad models with cellular data access built in, the same network used by modern cell phones. With cellular data enabled, your iPad likely has Internet access nearly everywhere.

note The iPad can hop onto a cellular network, but it can't place or receive calls like an iPhone. The cellular access is strictly for data. (You can still place calls using a service such as Skype or connect with others using FaceTime.)

However, cellular is more expensive: The cellular iPad models cost $130 more than the Wi-Fi–only models in the United States and require an additional fee to access the network. The good news is that Apple negotiated great deals with providers to provide cellular access. (Check with your carrier for specific pricing.)

note The iPad Air and Retina iPad mini contain all the hardware to connect to any cellular network; you no longer have to buy a specific model based on the carrier.

As you would expect, the pricing for plans is complicated—we are talking about cellular companies, after all, who profit on customer confusion—but there's a silver lining. In some cases, your iPad doesn't need to be tied to a multi-year service contract or existing plan. For my iPad Air, as an example, I pay a fixed monthly fee (about $30 as I write this) for 2 GB of cellular data use. (This price is current as of November 2013 and may have changed by the time you read this. Some providers also offer shared data plans for households that own several data devices.)

The great part of these deals is that, unlike with the iPhone, there's no contract that locks you in for a minimum length of time. Activate the plan when you need it (if you expect to travel a lot next month, for instance), and cancel when you're done. If you bump against the limit of one plan, you can jump to another plan or wait until the 30-day cycle begins again.

And you do it all from the iPad directly.

tip The cellular iPads boast a few other differences from the Wi-Fi models. For one, they include a GPS chip for identifying the iPad's position in Maps and other apps; the Wi-Fi models use a method based on wireless access points to determine location.

Understand cellular service

Here's a quick overview of the iPad's cellular capabilities. My apologies in advance for the alphabet soup here.

The iPad cellular models are capable of LTE (a meaningless acronym that stands for Long Term Evolution) data transfer, which can achieve up to 72 megabits per second (Mbps). If you're in a service area that offers LTE, that's the theoretical fastest transfer rate.

The cellular models also support three other varieties of cellular data: DC-HSDPA (42 Mbps), HSPA+ (21 Mbps), and HSPA (7.2 Mbps). To put these into context, the iPad 2 uses HSPA.

However, don't fret too much about these levels: The cellular iPad models will connect to the best signal that's available in your area, and fall back to 3G service if necessary.

Activate cellular service

To enable cellular service, do the following:

1. Go to Settings > Cellular Data and make sure the Cellular Data option is set to On (**Figure 1.18**).

Figure 1.18
Cellular Data preferences

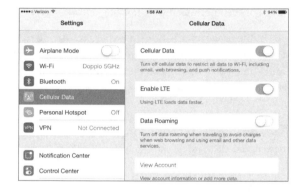

2. Tap the View Account button.

3. Tap the Set Up New Account button. (Depending on your cellular provider, you may also be able to add the iPad to an existing account.)

4. Enter your name, phone number, and email, and enter a password.

5. Tap a plan to choose it.

6. Enter your credit card and billing information and tap Next.

7. Read the terms of service and tap Agree.

8. Review the payment summary and tap Done.

As soon as a dialog appears informing you that the data service is activated, you can access the Internet anywhere you have cellular reception.

Measure your cellular data usage

So, just how far will you get with your data plan? As you might expect, that depends on your use. Go to Settings > Cellular Data and look at the Cellular Data Usage fields to view how much data has been sent and received. Tap the Reset Statistics button at the bottom of the screen to zero out the figures and start tracking anew.

To get the usage information from your provider, go to Settings > General > Cellular Data > View Account. The Account Overview section tells you how much data you've used, how much remains, and how many days are left in the billing period.

note   In an area where both Wi-Fi and cellular work, Wi-Fi supersedes the cellular network. Using the iPad at a Wi-Fi hotspot, for example, doesn't count toward the data limit even if cellular service is active.

Choose which apps can use cellular data

The Cellular Data settings also include a list of installed apps that can get data from the Internet. If you want to limit that capability—for example, to prevent FaceTime calls that would quickly eat up your allotted data— tap an app's switch to restrict it to using only Wi-Fi connections.

Add or cancel cellular service

As you approach the end of your allotted bandwidth, the iPad displays warnings when you reach 20 percent of data left, then 10 percent, and then zero. If you want to add bandwidth during one of those reminders, tap the Now button to bring up the Cellular Data Account window. You can also get there at any time by going to Settings > Cellular Data > View Account and tapping Add Data or Change Plan.

note International roaming data rates can be substantially higher than what your domestic carrier offers, so if you know you'll be traveling out of the country, tap the Add International Plan button and set up a plan.

Share the Internet connection using Personal Hotspot

The iPad is capable of acting like a portable Wi-Fi hotspot, sharing its cellular Internet access with up to five devices (such as your computer or a friend's iPad). The catch is that your cellular provider may not allow it, or may charge an extra fee. The connection can be shared via Wi-Fi, USB, or Bluetooth.

1. Go to Settings > Cellular Data > Personal Hotspot, and tap Set Up Personal Hotspot. After you enable the feature, a Personal Hotspot option appears on the first Settings screen.

2. Tap Personal Hotspot to view the settings, and then switch the feature to On.

3. On devices that want to connect, point them to the hotspot name (if sharing using Wi-Fi) and enter the password you set up in step 1.

tip The SIM card included with the iPad cellular models stores your name and account information. You can remove it from the iPad and put it into another device that accepts a nano SIM card and still use your account. It ships with a PIN that's set by the network provider. To lock the SIM card for added security, tap the SIM PIN button in the Cellular Data settings, switch SIM PIN to On, and enter 1111 (if that doesn't work, you need to contact your carrier to get the default unlock code). To set a new code, tap Change PIN and follow the instructions. (If you enter the wrong passcode three times, the SIM will be shut down and you'll need to contact the cellular provider to re-activate it. See http://support.apple.com/kb/HT4113 for more information.)

Use iCloud

iCloud is Apple's ambitious, ubiquitous service for keeping all of your data in sync no matter which computer or iOS device you're using. When you update some piece of information, such as an event in the Calendar app, the changes are copied to the iCloud servers and applied to every device that shares your iCloud account. You don't need to sync using a cable or via Wi-Fi; as long as you have a connection to the Internet, the information is updated automatically.

This feature is especially helpful when editing documents in apps that support iCloud. The file is copied wirelessly without fuss and kept up to date on all devices.

iCloud can sync email, contacts, calendar events, iOS reminders, Safari bookmarks, notes, music, and documents. For images, Photo Stream is a way to share new photos you capture using the iPad's camera, or to view photos you shoot with an iPhone or iPod touch or photos that are saved in compatible photo applications such as iPhoto.

Set up iCloud

If you didn't enable iCloud when you set up your iPad, do the following:

1. Open Settings > iCloud.

2. Enter your Apple ID and password.

3. Tap the Sign In button. The iPad verifies the information.

4. In the dialog that appears, allow iCloud to use location information for your iPad.

The iCloud settings include On/Off switches for the types of data that can be synced (**Figure 1.19**). Tap to enable or disable any of them. For the

Keychain, Photos, and Documents & Data options, tapping their names brings up additional options. (For example, Documents & Data lets you turn off cellular access for documents so you don't inadvertently chew up your cellular bandwidth allotment.)

Figure 1.19
iCloud settings

Sync data to iCloud

The beauty of iCloud is that once it's enabled, you don't have to do much else. Contacts and calendars, for instance, are automatically updated. Some items require a small amount of manual intervention. For example, music, TV shows, or apps you've purchased from the iTunes Store on a separate device can be downloaded to the iPad (see Chapter 8).

tip An option in iTunes lets you download new music, apps, books, and app updates to all of your devices when you purchase them. Go to Settings > iTunes & App Store and turn on the Automatic Downloads options for the media you want.

note You can also access your contacts, calendars, email, reminders, notes, and iWork documents using any modern Web browser at icloud.com. However, that works only on a computer, not on an iOS device.

iCloud backup

Instead of backing up the iPad's data to iTunes, you can back it up directly to iCloud when the iPad is connected to a Wi-Fi network and being charged. Go to Settings > iCloud > Storage & Backup and enable the iCloud Backup option. (You can also go to iTunes and, on the iPad's Summary screen, choose iCloud under Automatically Back Up.) Here you can also see how much of your free storage capacity is being used. As you might guess, Apple is happy to sell you more storage space.

Click the Manage Storage button to view which items are being stored and how much space they occupy. Some types of data stored on your iPad don't count against the free storage, such as Photo Stream images and purchased music, apps, books, and TV shows.

Use Notification Center

Under older versions of iOS, notifications were a hassle. If an app put up a notice, it appeared as a solitary box, obscuring everything else. In iOS 7, notifications are far more useful. You can read alerts, check your calendar, and access Notification Center even when the iPad is locked, for example.

You can read notifications by doing one of the following:

- Swipe down with one finger from the top of the screen to view Notification Center (**Figure 1.20**). The Today screen provides a snapshot of your day and the current weather. Tap the All button to view all notifications or the Missed button to see which ones appeared when you weren't using the iPad. Tap an item to go directly to it in the appropriate app. To hide the drawer, drag it back to the top of the screen.

- When a notification arrives as an alert, swipe the icon next to the message to jump directly to that app (**Figure 1.21**).

- While you're using the iPad, a new notification appears in a banner at the top of the screen. Tap it to view its app.

Figure 1.20
Notification Center

Figure 1.21
A Messages notification as an alert

tip Customize the appearance of notifications by going to Settings > Notifications. Tap an app name in the In Notification Center group to set a variety of preferences: whether new alerts show up as a banner at the top of the screen, show up as a dialog, or do not show up at all; how many items to show; whether new items appear as a badge on the app's icon; what sound to play when the notification arrives; whether to view it in the lock screen; and more, depending on the app. Here you can also decide in what order apps appear in Notification Center by tapping the Edit button and repositioning items in the list.

tip The banner notifications are mostly unintrusive, but sometimes they do get in the way. To dismiss one, quickly swipe up on the banner.

Activate Do Not Disturb

The problem with notifications, of course, is that they don't respect your schedule. I've been woken up a few times at 4 a.m. by well-meaning colleagues on the east coast who sent messages, not realizing my iPad would chime. The Do Not Disturb feature suppresses notifications and FaceTime calls, either when you manually enable the feature or during preset hours.

Go to Settings and switch the Do Not Disturb option to On. Or, bring up Control Center from the bottom of the screen and tap the Do Not Disturb button. You can tell it's active by the presence of a crescent moon in the menu bar (**Figure 1.22**).

Figure 1.22
Do Not Disturb enabled

To activate Do Not Disturb on a schedule, do the following:

1. Go to Settings > Do Not Disturb.

2. Turn the Scheduled option to On to reveal more settings (**Figure 1.23**).

Figure 1.23
*Do Not Disturb
options*

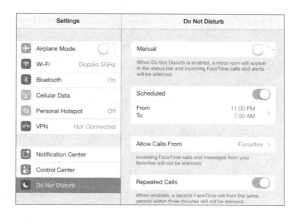

3. Tap the From/To button and set the start and end times for the Do Not Disturb range.

4. If you want to set up exceptions for incoming FaceTime calls, tap the Allow Calls From button and specify Everyone, No One, Favorites, or one of your groups from your contacts. In the event of an emergency, someone important may need to get through to you. (This feature is more appropriate on the iPhone for phone calls, but FaceTime is the closest thing on the iPad.)

A related setting, Repeated Calls, ensures that someone trying to get through by calling back quickly will get your attention.

note Do Not Disturb, at least in the iOS 7.0 release, does not apply when you're actively using the iPad. For example, if you're giving a presentation on the iPad, notifications can still appear. If you need to squelch the banners or alerts, you need to do it for each app that's likely to intrude (such as Messages, FaceTime, and Reminders). I also found that some notifications still slipped through.

Use Control Center

Control Center collects a host of controls that previously required you to dig through settings screens to access. No matter what app you're running, swipe up from the bottom of the screen to reveal Control Center (**Figure 1.24**). If you're in an app that's using the entire screen, such as when you're watching a movie in the Videos app, swipe once to reveal Control Center's tab, and then swipe again to reveal the controls.

Figure 1.24
Control Center

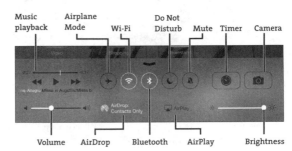

Labels above (left to right): Music playback, Airplane Mode, Wi-Fi, Do Not Disturb, Mute, Timer, Camera

Labels below (left to right): Volume, AirDrop, Bluetooth, AirPlay, Brightness

Connect to Bluetooth Devices

The iPad includes just two ports for connecting cables: the headphone port at the top and the dock port at the bottom. The rest of the iPad's communication happens wirelessly via Wi-Fi, cellular, or a third option: Bluetooth. Thanks to this short-range wireless technology, you can listen to music using Bluetooth headphones or speakers; you can also type using any Bluetooth keyboard instead of the onscreen keyboard or Apple's optional keyboard dock accessory.

 note When shopping for Bluetooth audio products, look for ones that support A2DP (Advanced Audio Distribution Profile). Also, the iPad mini and all iPads except the iPad 2 support the Bluetooth 4.0 protocol, a low-power version that works with devices that maintain long connections (such as some fitness trackers).

Pair the iPad and the device

To communicate with the iPad, a Bluetooth device must be *paired* with it to ensure that the device is recognized and won't get confused by other Bluetooth connections nearby. You need to pair the device only once, after which the iPad identifies and communicates with the keyboard or audio product automatically when it's within range. Follow these steps:

1. Open the Settings app and tap the Bluetooth option.

2. Slide the Bluetooth switch to On if it's not already on.

3. Power on the Bluetooth device you want to pair, and put it into its pairing mode; you may need to press and hold a button on the device to switch modes. It will appear in the Devices list (**Figure 1.25**).

Figure 1.25
*Paired and
unpaired devices*

4. If the iPad displays a dialog for pairing, skip to the next step. Otherwise, tap the name of the unpaired device.

5. Enter the device's PIN. For headsets, this is usually "0000" (four zeros), but check the device's instructions if that doesn't work. For keyboards, the PIN is a series of numbers that appears on the iPad screen.

If paired successfully, the device appears as Connected on the Bluetooth screen.

tip The iPad can be paired with more than one device at the same time. For example, you can listen to music through a wireless Bluetooth headset while typing on a Bluetooth keyboard.

tip When you're using a Bluetooth keyboard, the iPad's onscreen keyboard won't appear. This makes sense, except when you're close enough to be in range of the keyboard but not intending to use it. You may need to go into Settings and disable Bluetooth in that case (or turn off the keyboard's power, but is it really worth getting off the couch to do that?).

tip I bought the Apple Wireless Keyboard to use with my iPad, but you can use nearly any Bluetooth keyboard. When you want to turn off the Apple model without disabling Bluetooth on the iPad, press and hold the keyboard's power button for a few seconds until you see the status light disappear.

Forget the Bluetooth device

To remove a device from the list, tap the information button (ⓘ) and then tap the Forget this Device button.

Mirror Video

On the original iPad, the only way for teachers or presenters to share what was happening on the tablet's screen was to mount a camera above it and project the results. The iPad can mirror its video to an HDTV, digital projector, or other similar device. All you need is an Apple Digital AV Adapter or Apple VGA Adapter; plug it in and mirroring is automatically enabled. Better yet, if you also own an Apple TV, the iPad can mirror its screen over Wi-Fi. Here's how to activate it:

1. Swipe up from the bottom of the screen to reveal Control Center.

2. Tap the AirPlay button and choose the Apple TV on your network.

3. Set the Mirroring option to On (**Figure 1.26**).

Figure 1.26
*Start mirroring
the iPad's screen.*

 Here's a related use for your iPad that you may not have considered: Using Air Display by Avatron Software (www.avatron.com), you can make the iPad act as a second monitor for your computer. In fact, it can support up to four iPads simultaneously! Store chat windows, Photoshop tools, or anything else—the iPad's screen becomes a spanned extension of your computer's desktop.

Print Using AirPrint

It's fun to think we're living in a post-paper world where our news and books are delivered electronically and we can zap documents across the world in an instant. But, darn it, sometimes you just need a printed copy of something. AirPrint, the printing architecture built into iOS, does the job (provided you own a printer that supports AirPrint).

note See the following technote at Apple's site for a list of AirPrint-compatible printers: http://support.apple.com/kb/HT4356.

The act of printing is similar in all apps that support it, whether you're printing a message in Mail or a picture in the Photos app.

1. Tap the Share button (⬆). The button may vary depending on the app; in Mail, for example, the Print command is accessible by tapping the Reply button.

2. In the popover that appears, tap the Print button (**Figure 1.27**).

Figure 1.27
Find the Print button in the Share menu.

3. Tap the Printer button to choose a connected printer.

4. Choose the number of copies to print. This option may not always be available, depending on which app you're in and which printer you're printing to. Similarly, other options, such as double-sided printing, depend on the device.

5. Tap the Print button to print the document.

> **tip** Wait, don't give up on printing if you don't have one of the compatible printers! If you own a Mac, download Printopia (www.ecamm.com/mac/printopia/), which enables AirPrint to see printers that your computer can access. It also includes the ability to send a file to a Dropbox folder or directly to your Mac. If you run Windows, try the utility AirPrint Activator (www.macerkopf.de/airprint-ios-4-2-1-hack-fuer-windows-user-02481.html).

Search Using Spotlight

Even the smallest-capacity iPad model stores a lot of information. To locate something quickly, go to the Home screen and swipe down anywhere on the screen to reveal the Search field.

Type some text into the Search field to bring up results, sorted by apps (**Figure 1.28**). Tap the one you want to jump to. If you don't find what you're looking for, tap the Search Web or Search Wikipedia options at the bottom of the screen to view those search results in Safari. (You may have to hide the keyboard to view those two options if the search pulls up many results.)

Figure 1.28
*Spotlight
search results*

To quickly erase a term and start over, tap the cancel button (⊗) to the right of the Search field.

tip Spotlight also matches app names when you search, so if you have dozens of apps and don't want to navigate to the screen containing the one you want, simply perform a Spotlight search to locate and launch it (Figure 1.29).

Figure 1.29
I think I have a photo app problem.

2

Get and Use Apps

The iPad and iPad mini are sleek and shiny, fantastic examples of industrial design that packs a host of cutting-edge technologies into thin, responsive tablets. Aside from holding one in your hand, however, your time spent using the iPad will be focused almost entirely on its software.

The core apps that ship with the iPad are useful, but those are just the beginning. More than 1 million (at this writing) programs are available from the App Store, 475,000 of them made specifically for the iPad— so many that Apple's marketing tagline, "There's an app for that," has become part of current popular culture.

With a few taps (and often just a few dollars), you can locate, purchase, and download apps that do nearly anything you can think of. In this chapter, I tell you how to find and install apps, and also how you can share them with friends.

Find and Install Apps

Quick, jump in the car, let's go app shopping!

I almost had you there, didn't I? It used to be that buying a new program meant going to a store in the mall, or buying a box from an online retailer, or even downloading it from the developer directly. But that's not the case with iPad apps.

The only outlet to get apps is Apple's App Store, available on the iPad itself or from within iTunes. Pricing varies among apps, naturally, but most cost less than $15—in many cases, far less, with many apps available for free.

> **note** The App Store does not offer demo or shareware versions of apps, so it's difficult to evaluate an app before purchasing it. It's not impossible, though: Many vendors offer free "light" versions of their apps, which are limited in scope but give you a sense of what the paid version can do. Other apps may cost as little as $0.99 and offer just a handful of features, with the option to unlock others if you pony up some more cash.

The App Store on the iPad

Tap the App Store icon on the Home screen to launch the App Store. Since it's a storefront, you'll see many new and featured titles (**Figure 2.1**). To view more apps in boxed sections, such as Best New Apps, swipe left or right.

> **tip** It's sometimes difficult to get a sense of what an app offers by looking solely at screenshots, so be sure to tap the link that takes you to a developer's Web site for more information. Companies often include a video of how the app operates.

Figure 2.1
The App Store on the iPad

Swipe left or right to view more apps.

At the bottom of the screen, the buttons let you view featured apps; consult lists of the most popular paid and free apps in Top Charts; see apps installed by others in your geographic location; or access apps you've already purchased. (See "Update Apps," later in this chapter, for more about the Updates button.) If you already know what you're looking for, enter its name into the Search field in the upper-right corner of the screen.

To view more information about an app, including screenshots and customer reviews, tap its icon.

If you decide your life isn't complete without the app, tap the button that displays the price. The button changes to read Buy; if the app is free, you'll see "Install App" (**Figure 2.2**). Tap it again to purchase, or tap anywhere outside the button to switch back to the price.

Figure 2.2
*Purchasing
an app*

Tap the price to reveal
the Buy button.

After you enter your iTunes Store account password, the app downloads and is installed in the first open space on the Home screen (**Figure 2.3**).

Figure 2.3
*The app appears
on the Home
screen and is
automatically
installed.*

note If you're connected to the Internet using cellular networking, large apps—over 50 MB—won't be downloaded. Connect to a Wi-Fi network or use iTunes on your computer and try the purchase again. Waiting for Wi-Fi also means you won't chew up your monthly cellular data allotment with app update downloads.

tip The iTunes Store knows which apps you've purchased in the past (for the Apple ID you're signed in with). Those appear with an iCloud button (⬇); no need to re-buy them.

The App Store within iTunes on a computer

If you're on your computer, you can purchase apps in iTunes and then
sync them to the iPad later. However, an extra step is required when
buying apps. Fire up iTunes, click the iTunes Store button, and then click
the App Store heading at the top. After clicking the Buy button, the app
is downloaded and added to iTunes. When you next perform a sync, the
app is transferred to the iPad and appears on the Home screen. That said,
I almost never need to install apps. Read on...

Automatically install purchased apps

If you already own another iOS device, such as an iPhone, it's likely you
want new apps to appear on the iPad as well. Normally you'd have
to download a purchased app again on the iPad or sync with iTunes
(provided you've synced the iPhone first). Instead, you can opt to automatically download new apps, music, and books.

Go to Settings > iTunes & App Store and turn on the Automatic Downloads option for Apps. A similar preference exists in the settings for
iTunes, categorized under the Store heading.

Run iPhone apps on the iPad

You'll find apps that are written specifically for the iPad, but your iPad
can also run apps written for both the iPhone and iPod touch. In some
cases, a single app can run on all three devices—the app contains
resources that take advantage of the iPad when run there, but that
are ignored when run on an iPhone or iPod touch.

Apps not adapted to the iPad work in one of two ways: either at their
actual size centered in the screen, or enlarged to fill the screen. Tap the 2x
button in the upper-right corner to scale the app to fill the screen, or tap
the 1x button to return to the original size.

Update Apps

When developers update their software, they submit a changed version to the App Store, where Apple approves the update and makes it available. Because everything goes through the App Store, your iPad can check for updates so you don't have to go searching for them online.

A numbered badge appears on the App Store icon in the Home screen, indicating how many updates are ready to be downloaded (**Figure 2.4**). In iTunes, the badge appears on the Apps item in the sidebar.

Figure 2.4
*App updates
are available.*

Badge on
App Store icon

note   You don't have to wait for the iPad or iTunes to communicate with the Apple mothership. In the App Store app, tap the Updates button to trigger a check for new versions. In iTunes, select the Apps item in the sidebar and then click the Check for Updates button.

To install the updates on the iPad, do the following:

1. Tap the App Store app to launch it.

2. Tap the Updates button in the bottom toolbar. A list of updated apps appears.

3. To learn more about the update, tap its name in the list. Otherwise, skip to the next step.

4. Tap the Update button next to any single app you want to download.

   Or, tap the Update All button at the top of the screen to download and install all updates at once.

tip A scary-looking dialog may appear before the download begins, warning that an app may contain material inappropriate for children. Apple is strict about the type of content that's accepted into the App Store, so you shouldn't find anything too suggestive, and certainly nothing explicit. However, Apple can't control all content, especially for apps that fetch data from the Web, so the company throws up this disclaimer.

A new feature of iOS 7 is the ability to automatically update apps in the background. If you find that you don't often check for updates, or you can't stand to see the little red badge on the App Store icon, go to Settings > iTunes & App Store and activate the Updates switch under Automatic Downloads.

What if you want to re-download an app you purchased, but you can't remember its exact name? In the App Store app, tap the Purchased button to view your purchase history and download any apps that aren't currently installed on the iPad.

Remove Apps

As you download more apps—and I predict you will—you're going to find that some don't hold the allure they once did, or you'll discover a new app that does something better than the first one you downloaded. You can remove the app on the iPad itself or disable it from syncing within iTunes.

On the iPad

1. Locate the app you want to remove on the Home screen, and then touch and hold its icon for a second. All of the apps begin to shake, and an X button appears on the app's icon.

2. Tap the X button.

3. Tap the Delete button in the confirmation dialog that appears
   (**Figure 2.5**).

Figure 2.5
Remove an app from the iPad.

Tap here to delete. ──

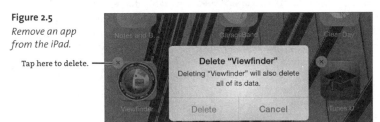

The original apps that ship with the iPad cannot be removed. If they're
in your way, consider moving them to another Home screen or into a
folder (described in "Customize the Home Screen," coming up).

In iTunes

1. Connect the iPad to your computer and select its name in the iTunes
   sidebar.

2. Click the Applications tab in the main section of the screen.

3. Locate the app you wish to remove, either in the list of applications or
   in the preview area of the different Home screens (**Figure 2.6**).

Figure 2.6
Remove an app in iTunes.

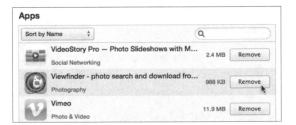

4. Position your mouse pointer over the app you wish to remove and click the X button. Or, in the list, click the checkbox to the left so that it is not marked.

5. Click the Apply button to pass the changes along to the iPad. iTunes asks you to confirm that you want to remove the app, and if you click Yes, the iPad syncs.

Share Apps

Apps you've downloaded can be loaded onto any other iPad, iPad mini, iPhone, or iPod touch that you sync with your computer. But what you may not know is that you can share apps with up to five other computers (including friends' computers) using the Home Sharing feature of iTunes.

For example, let's say I want to play a game of Scrabble for iPad with my wife. Here's how to get the app I purchased onto her iPad.

1. Make sure your friend's computer is on the same local network as your computer.

2. Enable Home Sharing in both computers by choosing File > Home Sharing > Turn On Home Sharing (if it's already active, skip to step 5).

3. Enter your iTunes account name (the email address you use for purchasing things from the iTunes Store) and password, and then click the Create Home Share button. Be sure to use the same account (yours, since you are sending the app) on both computers.

4. If iTunes asks to authorize the computer, click Yes.

5. On your friend's computer, click the Library button (at the top left, below the playback controls) and choose the name of your library listed under Home Shares.

6. After the library has loaded, click the Library button again—which in my example reads "Music (Jeff's MBP Library)"—and choose Apps.

7. Select the app you want to transfer. For help locating the app, go to the Show pop-up menu in the lower-left corner and choose Items Not in My Library.

8. Click the Import button (**Figure 2.7**). The app file copies to your friend's iTunes library. He or she can then sync the iPad to install the app.

Figure 2.7
Importing an app from another copy of iTunes

App on my computer to be imported

note Because your friend didn't purchase the app originally, she needs to enter your iTunes password to update the app. If you trust your friend enough to give her your password, that's not a problem, but it also means she can buy anything from the iTunes Store on your dime.

Set App Preferences

Every app has its own settings, but finding them can be scattershot. Many apps include preferences within the app itself, so you can do everything in one place. Apple's recommended (and awkward, in my opinion) method is to put preferences within the Settings app (**Figure 2.8**). Scroll to the bottom of the Settings screen to view apps, then tap an app's name to access its preferences.

Figure 2.8

App-specific preferences in the Settings app

Customize the Home Screen

I introduced the Home screen in Chapter 1 and mentioned how you can swipe each screenful of apps to find what you're looking for. What I didn't mention was that you can move the apps between screens and organize apps into folders, so you don't have to swipe several times to get to a frequently used app that appears on the last screen. It's also possible to change the background image to personalize your iPad.

On the iPad

1. Touch and hold any app for a second until the apps begin to shake.

2. Drag an app you want to move to a different position on the screen. Or, to move an app to another screen, drag it to the left or right edge of the screen and hold it there.

   After a moment, the screen advances and you still have control over positioning the app.

3. Lift your finger to drop the app in place.

4. Press the Home button to return to the Home screen's normal mode.

tip The apps in the Dock at the bottom of each Home screen remain the same, no matter which screen you're viewing. Put your most frequently used apps there.

Organize apps into folders

On the original iPad, my apps were strewn across nine Home screens. I moved my most frequently used apps to the first two or three screens, but even then I got sick of swiping to access apps. Now, my iPad is down to three Home screens, thanks to the ability to put related apps into groups that Apple calls folders. Earlier versions imposed a limit of 12 apps in a folder (16 if you owned an iPhone 5), but that ceiling is gone in iOS 7. You could put all of your apps in a single folder if you choose (or if you want to play a prank on someone).

1. Touch and hold an app you want to move, until all of the app icons are shaking.

2. Drag an app *onto the top* of another app. After a moment, the screen zooms in to a "folder"—a container holding the apps (**Figure 2.9**).

Figure 2.9
App added to a folder group

3. A name for the folder is automatically assigned based on the categories of the apps, but you can change it. Select the text field and type your own title.

4. Drag other apps onto a folder icon to add them to it.

5. Press the Home button to finish rearranging the icons.

When you want to access an app within a folder, tap the folder to expose its contents and then tap the app you wish to open.

tip Maybe you don't want to swipe between Home screens at all. You can just as easily create a folder of apps and then put the folder in the Dock at the bottom of the screen. That approach lets you access apps from the Dock alone, plus 20 more on the first Home screen!

In iTunes

1. Connect the iPad to your computer, select it from the Devices list, and go to the Apps tab.

2. Double-click one of the Home screens to edit it. Or, scroll down to access the folders you've created (**Figure 2.10**).

Figure 2.10
Editing Home screens in iTunes

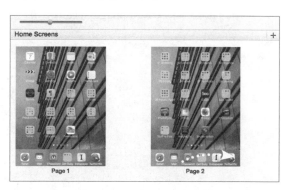

3. Drag an app to a new location, including to other screens, which are displayed in the right-hand column.

To create a folder, drag an app onto another app; or drag an app to an existing folder.

You can also drag an entire Home screen in that column to a different location. This is great if, for example, you keep games on one screen and business apps on another and want to change their order.

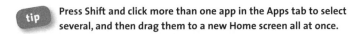 **tip** Press Shift and click more than one app in the Apps tab to select several, and then drag them to a new Home screen all at once.

4. Click the Apply button to sync the changes to the iPad.

Change the Home screen image

The iPad includes many alternate Home screen images, or you can use one of your own photos as the background. You can also set the image that comes up when you unlock the iPad.

1. Go to Settings > Wallpapers & Brightness.

2. Tap the Choose Wallpaper button (which displays your current lock and Home screens) to view images (**Figure 2.11**).

Figure 2.11
*Choose an album
of wallpaper
images.*

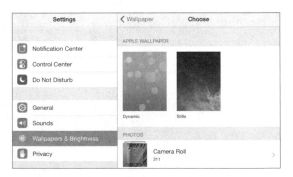

3. Tap an image to select it and to see a preview of how it will appear.

4. If the image is larger than the iPad's screen resolution (which includes most digital photos), you can refine its appearance. Resize it by using pinch and expand gestures, and reposition it by dragging with one finger.

5. Tap the Set Lock Screen, Set Home Screen, or Set Both button to make the change (**Figure 2.12**). Or, tap Cancel to choose a different image.

Figure 2.12
Set the wallpaper.

3

Browse the Web

Web browsers on smartphones were historically pretty terrible. The iPhone lets you view sites without having to load a stripped-down alternate version, but even though Safari on the iPhone *can* render a page as it would appear in a desktop Web browser, the screen size is still a limitation, which is why many sites serve up mobile versions. (Sometimes a mobile site is done well, but too often it's painful.)

The iPad and iPad mini, on the other hand, are almost all screen, with a version of Safari that displays Web sites just as you'd see them on a Mac or Windows PC. We no longer wonder or marvel at how we access information online—we just get it.

Access Web Sites

Tap the Safari icon on the Home screen to launch the iPad's Web browser. I'm assuming you have an active Internet connection, either via Wi-Fi or cellular. If not, go back to Chapter 1 for a refresher on getting online.

note As soon as you try to access a Web site in Safari, the program checks for an Internet connection. If one isn't found, the iPad asks if you want to join a nearby Wi-Fi network.

Open and read a new Web page

Safari opens to a new page containing icons of Favorites—either Safari's default selection or, if you enabled iCloud during the setup process (see Chapter 1), Favorites you've set up.

1. Tap the smart search field at the top of the screen.

2. Enter the address of the site you want to visit.

   To quickly erase what you've typed and start over, tap the cancel button (⊗) at the right edge of the field.

   As you type, Safari suggests matching URLs from your bookmarks or history.

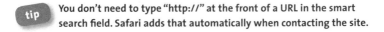

tip You don't need to type "http://" at the front of a URL in the smart search field. Safari adds that automatically when contacting the site.

3. Tap the Go key in the onscreen keypad, or tap a suggested address. After a few seconds, the page appears (**Figure 3.1**).

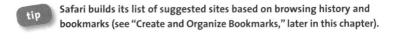

tip Safari builds its list of suggested sites based on browsing history and bookmarks (see "Create and Organize Bookmarks," later in this chapter).

Back/Next Share Smart search field Bookmarks   iCloud Tabs New

Figure 3.1
*A new Safari
window*

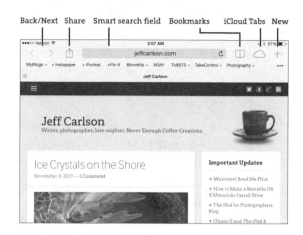

To read the site's content, flick or drag the page in any direction to scroll it. If you'd like to enlarge an area, double-tap that spot to zoom in—Safari smartly figures out how much zoom to apply based on the page's layout. You can also spread two fingers to enlarge manually. Double-tap or pinch to zoom back out.

 To quickly jump to the top of a Web page, tap the status bar at the top of the screen. (This shortcut works in most apps.)

To follow a link to another page, simply tap the text or image that is linked. You can return to the previous page by tapping the Back button in the toolbar.

Reload or cancel

Tap the icon at the right edge of the address bar (↻) to reload the page. While the content is downloading, the icon becomes a cancel button (✕); tap it if you want to stop loading.

Read uncluttered pages using Reader

Even with the high-resolution display of the Retina iPad, text can be small on some Web sites, and sometimes there are so many ads and other distractions that it can be difficult to read an article. Safari's Reader feature can cut through the clutter.

1. Open a Web page that contains an article of some sort. Safari is pretty smart about differentiating between a page with content and a home page with lots of links.

2. Tap the Reader button that appears in the smart search bar to view the article in a highly readable overlay (**Figure 3.2**). (If you don't see a Reader button, you probably aren't viewing a single article; tap a link for the item you want to read.)

3. When you're done reading, tap the Reader button again.

Figure 3.2
The Reader view

Reader button ——

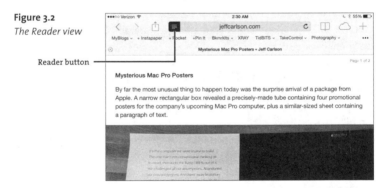

tip Want to change the size of the text? Safari supports the Dynamic Type feature in iOS, which scales text throughout the system. Go to Settings > General > Text Size and drag the slider to increase or decrease the text. For even bigger text, go to Settings > General > Accessibility > Larger Type and enable the Larger Dynamic Type setting.

View your browsing history

What if you want to view a Web page you loaded yesterday? If you know the site's address, you could start typing it and pick it from the list of possible matches. Or, you could view the entire list of sites you've visited.

1. Tap the Bookmarks button in the toolbar.

2. Tap the History button at the top of the popover that appears (**Figure 3.3**).

3. Tap the name of the site you visited.

Figure 3.3
Viewing your browsing history

Open new pages

To open a new page, do one of the following:

- Tap the New Tab (+) button at the right of the tab bar. An empty Safari window appears, where you can enter an address or perform a search.

- Another option is to open a link in a new page. Instead of just tapping the link, touch and hold it, and then tap Open in New Tab (**Figure 3.4**).

Figure 3.4
Touch and hold a link to open it in a new tab.

Bringing up the popover also reveals the link's URL and gives you the option to copy it to the iPad's memory for pasting elsewhere (such as in an outgoing Mail message).

With several pages open at the same time, switch between them by tapping the tab that belongs to the one you want to view.

 When you open a new tab from a link, by default it opens in the background, keeping you on the page you're reading. You can change the behavior so that the new tab is immediately brought forward: Go to Settings > Safari and turn off the Open New Tabs in Background option.

Access pages on other devices using iCloud Tabs

I access the Web on my iPad, my iPhone, and my Mac, and on each machine I tend to have different windows open. But what if I want to read something on my iPad that's open on my Mac? iCloud Tabs syncs and shares the addresses of all pages open on all devices.

Tap the iCloud Tabs button to view pages open on your other devices that share your iCloud account, and then tap a site to visit (**Figure 3.5**).

Figure 3.5
iCloud Tabs

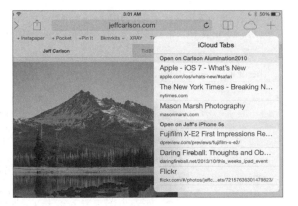

View links using Shared Links

The bulk of my interesting reading arrives via Twitter these days, as friends and acquaintances post links to articles and other miscellany. I could scroll through my tweet stream looking for things, or I could take advantage of the Shared Links feature in Safari. Tap the Bookmarks button and then tap the Shared Links (@) button to view only tweets that contain Web addresses (**Figure 3.6**). Tap one to follow the link.

Figure 3.6
Shared Links

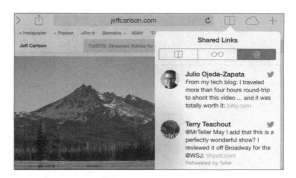

Watch videos

Many videos that appear on Web pages can be viewed within Safari (unless they're delivered using Flash, which the iPad doesn't support). A play button appears on videos you can watch (**Figure 3.7**).

Figure 3.7
Embedded video

Button indicates you can play this video.

Tap the button to begin playing the video. When you do, the iPad's video controls appear (**Figure 3.8**).

Figure 3.8
Playing embedded video

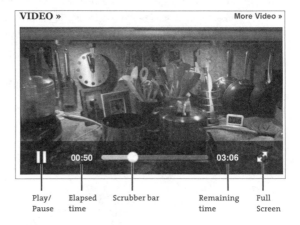

Play/ Pause   Elapsed time   Scrubber bar   Remaining time   Full Screen

The scrubber bar displays the video's progress; the light gray portion to the right of the playhead indicates how much of the video has been downloaded. To jump ahead in the movie, drag the playhead across the scrubber bar. Tap the Full Screen button to enlarge the video to use the entire iPad screen, hiding the rest of the Web page. You may also see an AirPlay button, which would send the video to an AirPlay-compatible device such as an Apple TV (see Chapter 8 for more on AirPlay).

> **tip** You can also use a two-fingered expand gesture (moving your fingers apart) on the movie to quickly zoom it into full-screen mode. Once there, double-tap the video to switch between viewing the full width of the movie (with black bars) and filling the screen (which crops the image).

Close pages

When you no longer wish to keep a Web page open, tap the X button to the left of the title in its tab.

Search the Web

What did we do before we could search the Internet for everything? How did we win trivia bets with our friends or recall specific movie quotes (and other important things, I'm sure)? You can navigate to any search engine's Web site, but it's easier to perform the search directly from the toolbar.

Tap the smart search field in Safari and start typing your search term (**Figure 3.9**). Tap one of the suggested terms that appear as you type; or, tap the Go key in the onscreen keyboard to go to Google's results page.

Figure 3.9
Searchin' Safari

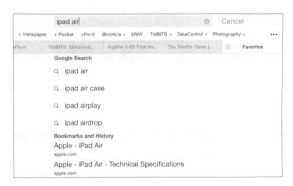

> **tip** Safari uses Google as its default search engine, but you can also choose to set Yahoo or Bing as the source for the search field. Go to Settings > Safari > Search Engine, and choose Google, Yahoo, or Bing.

Search within a Web page

What good is a search engine if, when you bring up the Web page that contains your search term, it's impossible to find the term? Safari searches within the contents of a Web page, too.

1. With a page loaded, enter your term in the search field. The first results lead to searches elsewhere on the Web, but the bottom of the list includes an On This Page section (provided there are matches).

2. Tap the Find "[the term]" option. The first instance is highlighted.

3. At the bottom of the screen, tap the Next button to highlight the next instance (**Figure 3.10**).

4. To look for something else on the page, enter the term in the search field in the lower bar. Or, tap Done to stop searching.

Figure 3.10
Searching within the page

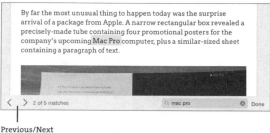

By far the most unusual thing to happen today was the surprise arrival of a package from Apple. A narrow rectangular box revealed a precisely-made tube containing four promotional posters for the company's upcoming Mac Pro computer, plus a similar-sized sheet containing a paragraph of text.

2 of 5 matches   mac pro   Done

Previous/Next

note You're not limited to using Safari's default search field. In addition to going to any search engine's Web site, several standalone search apps are available, such as Microsoft's Bing and, yes, even Google. They typically add other features not available in a Web browser; for example, Google Search offers a voice search capability that competes with Siri.

Read Pages Later with Reading List

In an ideal world, I'd sit all day and read the dozens of interesting articles and Web sites that I run across on Twitter, Facebook, email, and other outlets. Instead, I live in the real world, but I can offload a lot of that reading until it's more convenient by using Safari's Reading List. It remembers the link of a Web page so you can load the page later. To add a page to Reading List, do the following:

1. With a page loaded that you want to read later, tap the Share button to the left of the address field.

2. Tap the Add to Reading List button. The page and its information is saved and automatically shared to your other devices via iCloud.

When you're ready to read the page on the iPad, tap the Bookmarks button and then tap the Reading List button at the bottom of the popover. You can list everything you've saved or just pages you haven't read (**Figure 3.11**). Tap a page to load it.

Figure 3.11
*Items added to
Reading List*

 Go to Settings > Safari to find a Reading List setting called **Use Cellular Data**. When that option is enabled, items in the Reading List update even if you're not on a Wi-Fi connection. Turn it off to make sure Reading List isn't using your cellular data allotment when you're out of Wi-Fi range.

 To delete an item from Reading List, swipe left to right and then tap the Delete button.

Create and Organize Bookmarks

A Web browser is a great reference tool, not just because there are more than 1 trillion Web pages on the Internet (Google's estimate in 2008), but because you can store bookmarks for sites that you want to visit later. Safari on the iPad can create bookmarks and also use the bookmarks you've created on your computer.

Open a bookmarked page

Apple includes a few basic bookmarks in Safari, which will give us a sense of how opening a bookmark works. Tap the Bookmarks button on the toolbar, and then tap the name of a Web page from the list to load it.

 tip Here's a handy bookmark: Apple includes a Web version of the iPad User Guide at the bottom of the Bookmarks list.

Create a new bookmark

When you find a page you want to return to later, do the following:

1. Tap the Share button in the toolbar.

2. In the popover that appears, tap the Add Bookmark button.

3. Edit the name of the bookmark, if you wish (**Figure 3.12**).

Figure 3.12
Create a bookmark.

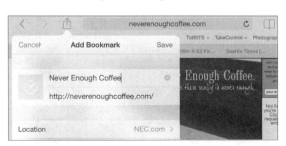

4. Tap the Location button and choose where the bookmark will be located in the Bookmarks hierarchy.

Typically, there are just two levels to the hierarchy: the Bookmarks folder itself and the Bookmarks Bar, a subfolder whose contents appear as tappable shortcuts beneath the toolbar.

5. Tap the Save button to create the bookmark.

tip I store nearly all of my active bookmarks on the Bookmarks Bar, organized in Safari on my Mac. For that reason, I choose to make the Bookmarks Bar always visible in Safari (normally it appears only when you're typing in the address or search field). To do this, go to Settings > Safari and enable the Always Show Bookmarks Bar option.

Edit a bookmark

Suppose you realize that your bookmark's name is too long to fit with other bookmarks on the Bookmarks Bar, or you want to put it into a different subfolder. Here's how to edit existing bookmarks on the iPad.

1. Tap the Bookmarks button on the toolbar and tap the identical Bookmarks button at the bottom of the popover that appears (if it's not already selected).

2. Locate the bookmark you want to edit; this could mean tapping a subfolder (like Bookmarks Bar) to view its contents.

3. Tap the Edit button at the bottom of the the popover. The items in the list gain red icons to the left of their names (**Figure 3.13**).

Figure 3.13
Editing the Bookmarks list

4. Edit the bookmark in any of the following ways:

   - To reposition the item within the list, touch the icon at the far right and drag it to a new spot.

   - Tap the bookmark name to change the title or URL. This is also where you can move the bookmark to another subfolder by tapping the button at the bottom of the popover. Use the navigation button at the top of the popover to return to the enclosing folder, or simply tap anywhere outside it to apply the change.

   - To remove a bookmark, tap the red icon to the left of its name, which displays a Delete button to the right. Tap that Delete button to remove the bookmark. (This two-step process is designed to avoid accidentally deleting bookmarks.)

5. Tap the Done button to exit the editing mode.

 A faster method of deleting bookmarks is to swipe left-to-right across the item's name to bring up the Delete button.

Add a Web page to the Home screen

What if you want to jump to a frequently viewed Web page more quickly than navigating bookmarks? Create a Home screen icon for it.

1. In Safari, navigate to the page you want to bookmark.

2. Tap the Share button.

3. Tap the Add to Home Screen button.

4. In the popover that appears, edit the icon's name (**Figure 3.14**).

5. Tap the Add button. The new icon appears on the Home screen. Tapping that icon opens the Web page in a new Safari window.

Figure 3.14
*Creating a
Home screen icon*

Editing the name

Icon on
Home screen

Share a page via AirDrop

When someone with a recent iOS device is nearby, you can send a Web site to them using AirDrop, Apple's technology for short-range discovery and communication. (See Chapter 10 for information on how to set up AirDrop.) Tap the Share button and then select the icon of a device near you to send the current page (**Figure 3.15**).

Figure 3.15
*Sending a Web
page via AirDrop*

A nearby device (my iPhone) has AirDrop
enabled and appears at the top.

The page is received on
the iPhone.

note   Although both iOS and OS X have features named AirDrop, it's not currently possible to share items from iPad to Mac or vice versa. I say "currently" because I find it hard to believe that Apple would use the same name on both platforms without a plan to make them work together at some point in the future.

Share a page's address via email

For a traditional approach, you can easily share a Web page with someone by sending them a link via email. Tap the Share button, and tap the
Mail button in the popover. A new outgoing email appears with the page
title already entered into the Subject field and the link in the body. All
you have to do is enter a recipient's email address and tap Send.

Share a page via Twitter or Facebook

Twitter and Facebook, once enclaves for geeks and college students, are
now massive social networking behemoths that enable you to publish
text snippets or media that can be read by anyone who follows your
account or accesses it on the Web.

Apple supports Twitter and Facebook at the system level, making it easy
to share information with your friends and followers without requiring
a dedicated app. (Set up your account information in Settings > Twitter,
and Settings > Facebook.)

In this case, if you run across a Web page you think others would like,
you can share its address directly from within Safari.

1. Tap the Share button and tap the Twitter or Facebook button.

2. In the dialog that appears, enter text that will accompany the Web
   address. Optionally, tap the Add Location button if you want to share
   your current physical location. When sharing to Facebook, you can also
   choose your audience (Public, Friends, or groups to which you belong.)

3. Tap Send to post the message to your account.

Expand Safari's Capabilities with Bookmarklets

Safari supports JavaScript, a scripting language that offers all sorts of interactivity on the Web, including *bookmarklets*—tiny bookmarks that use JavaScript code instead of a Web site address. What does that mean for non-developers? It adds features that Safari lacks.

For example, one of my favorite iPad and iPhone apps is Instapaper (www.instapaper.com). When I'm viewing a Web page that I want to read later—a long article, for example—I tap a "Read Later" book-marklet that Instapaper created in my Bookmarks Bar, which adds the page to my Instapaper account. Later, in the Instapaper app, I can read the page without being online, and in a format that strips out all the junk surrounding most Web pages (**Figure 3.16**). (Many third-party apps include Instapaper support natively, avoiding the need to take a side trip to Safari and activate a bookmarklet.)

Figure 3.16
The same article in Safari and Instapaper

Safari   Instapaper

To find more, search for "bookmarklet" in your favorite search engine and explore.

AutoFill Forms

How many Web sites do you visit that require some sort of account? There's no way I can keep track of all the logins and passwords for various news, travel, and shopping sites. One option is to simply use the same password for everything, but that's dangerous. If someone were to discover that password, they'd have access to all of your sites.

Safari's AutoFill feature can keep track of those credentials for you and give you the option of filling in the information with one tap.

tip While we're talking about security, allow me to recommend 1Password (www.agilebits.com), a great secure repository for all of your logins and other sensitive information. 1Password exists as an application for the Mac or Windows, and as an app for the iPad/iPhone/iPod touch. On my Mac it's essential, letting me easily fill in logins and storing new logins as I create them. It can also keep my credit card information handy for when I'm making purchases. The mobile app can't tie directly into Safari (due to restrictions imposed by Apple on sharing data between apps), but it's very handy when I need to look up a login. The best part: If you have both the iOS app and the desktop version, you can sync your logins between the computer and the device.

Enable AutoFill

Before we start capturing passwords, we need to make sure AutoFill is turned on.

1. Go to Settings > Safari > Passwords & AutoFill.

2. Toggle the switch for Names and Passwords to On.

3. If you want Safari to fill in personal information such as your name and address in forms, to save you from typing it all, enable the Use Contact Info option. Tap My Info to locate the entry for yourself in the Contacts app (see Chapter 10 for more information).

Store a new login

The first time you fill out a form, you have the option to save it.

1. When you tap a form field, the onscreen keyboard appears with buttons for jumping to the Previous or Next field (which is often easier than moving your fingers from the keyboard and tapping the next or previous field on the page) and for using AutoFill (**Figure 3.17**).

Figure 3.17
Filling in a form

Previous/Next
field buttons

2. Type the relevant information in the fields.

3. Tap the Go button in the onscreen keyboard, or tap the button that submits the data on the Web page (which may be labeled Submit, Log In, Go, or any number of other terse verbs).

4. In the dialog that appears, choose one of the following:

   - **Save Password:** Save the password for later. The next time you visit, the name and password will automatically be filled in.

   - **Never for This Website:** Do not save the password, and never ask about saving it for this site in the future. I use this option when accessing sensitive sites such as my bank, where I'd prefer to manually enter the password each time.

   - **Not Now:** Ignore AutoFill for now, but allow Safari to ask you about it next time.

iCloud Keychain

I mentioned 1Password two pages back as a place to store all of your passwords, but as of iOS 7 it's not the only solution. When iCloud Keychain is enabled in your iCloud settings, Safari can suggest secure passwords and store them for use on all of your devices and on Macs running OS X Mavericks (iCloud Keychain isn't offered under Windows; Chapter 11 details setting up the feature). To use it in Safari, do the following:

1. Enter a Password field (such as on a site's sign-up form) and tap the Suggest Password button above the onscreen keyboard.

2. In the dialog that appears, Safari creates a secure password; to use it, tap the Use Suggested Password button (**Figure 3.18**). Safari fills in the field (and a Confirm Password field if present).

Figure 3.18
Safari suggests a secure password.

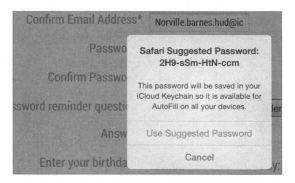

The next time you sign in to that site, Safari can automatically fill in the password it created.

AutoFill contact information

When you encounter a form that asks for your personal information,
tap one of the fields to bring up the keyboard and then tap the AutoFill
button. The data from your Contacts entry appears (**Figure 3.19**).

Figure 3.19
*Using AutoFill
for contact
information*

AutoFill items
appear in yellow.

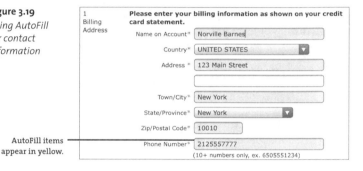

Maintain Web Privacy

Safari offers many options designed to limit how your data is used.

Private browsing

This mode prevents Safari from storing your browsing history and revealing any other personal information. To enable it, open a new tab in Safari
and tap the Private button at the bottom of the screen or just above the
onscreen keyboard when it's visible; you're asked if you want to keep or
close any open tabs. To turn off the Private option, tap the smart search
bar in any tab to display the keyboard (or open a new tab) and tap
Private again.

Privacy settings

Use the following options in Settings > Safari to fine-tune Web privacy:

- **Block Pop-ups:** Prevent sites from automatically loading new browser windows, which are usually annoying ads.

- **Do Not Track:** Safari sends a request that sites do not track your browsing activities (used mostly by advertisers). The site must support the feature to honor the request, however. (I just leave this on.)

- **Block Cookies:** By default, Safari only stores cookies—small bits of code that save some preferences or track your visit—created by sites you visit. You can also choose to never or always accept cookies.

- **Smart Search Field:** The options here allow search engines to feed suggestions as you type and to load the top search hit in the background for speedier loading.

- **Fraudulent Website Warning:** If you follow a link to a site that's known to be a security risk, Safari gives you a warning and the option to continue.

- **Clear History:** Tap this button to erase your entire browsing history. This feature is also available as a button in the navigation bar when you're viewing the History folder from the Bookmarks list.

- **Clear Cookies and Data:** In addition to cookies, Safari stores the contents of recent Web pages so that if you return to a site, it doesn't need to re-download images and other data that may not have changed. If you see a Web page that doesn't seem to have changed its content, try tapping this option to clear Safari's data cache and force a reload.

- **Website Data:** Tap Advanced to access this feature, which allows you to erase any data that sites have stored on your iPad.

- **JavaScript:** If you're concerned that a site may be using JavaScript to do something nefarious (like masquerade as a legitimate site), you can turn JavaScript off in the Advanced options.

4

Communicate Using Mail and Messages

Email is a prime candidate for liberation from the desktop. A lot of what I do occurs via email, whether I'm corresponding with friends and relatives or tossing around ideas for upcoming projects. But there's no reason all of that has to happen in front of a desktop or laptop.

Using the Mail app on the iPad, you can quickly read and reply to messages and dash off notes you may have otherwise ignored because of the hassle of doing it on the computer. Mail also handles incoming file attachments, making it a gateway for sending and receiving files.

Sometimes, though, even email is overkill or too slow when you want to just send a quick note to someone. The Messages app brings instant messaging—a feature usually found on cell phones—to the iPad. And as long as the recipient also has a device running Messages, the texts you send are free (not charged the exorbitant rates of SMS messages).

Set Up Mail

Most likely, you already have email accounts set up on the computer you use to sync with the iPad. You can also set up an account on the iPad itself—for example, you may want to use an iCloud account on the iPad for personal mail that isn't synced to a work computer.

Sync mail accounts from a computer

Mail accounts you've set up under Windows—in Outlook 2010, Outlook 2007, Outlook 2003, or Outlook Express—appear in iTunes. The same applies to accounts in the Mail application in older versions of OS X.

note   Apple does not support this method of syncing under OS X Mavericks, since it relies on an outdated feature called Sync Services. If you don't see an Info tab, you're probably running Mavericks.

1. With the iPad connected to your computer, select its name in the sidebar and then click the Info tab.

2. Select the checkbox for Sync Mail Accounts, and then enable accounts you wish to access on the iPad.

3. Click the Sync button. The accounts' settings are added to the iPad's Mail app. Syncing transfers only the account settings, not any of the messages on your computer.

Set up an account on the iPad

It's easy to add an account directly on the iPad. Mail can automatically configure accounts from iCloud, Gmail, Yahoo Mail, and AOL, as well as Microsoft Exchange accounts, provided you have your account name and password.

note   The options on the iPad apply only to email accounts you've previously created. If you want to sign up for a new service—say, a new Gmail account—you need to do that on your computer or using Safari on the iPad.

1. Go to Settings > Mail, Contacts, Calendars.

2. Under the Accounts heading, tap the Add Account button.

3. Tap a service name that matches your account.

   If you get your email from a different provider, tap the Other button and then tap the Add Mail Account button.

4. Enter a name for the account, the email address, and the password (**Figure 4.1**). The Description field automatically fills in the name of the service, but you can edit it separately if you prefer.

Figure 4.1
Enter account information.

5. Tap the Next button. The system verifies the information.

   If you're setting up an Other account, enter the account type (IMAP or POP) and the incoming and outgoing mail server information that your provider gave you when you signed up.

6. For services that support it, you can also set up over-the-air syncing of contacts, calendars, and notes. Make any of those services available by tapping their On buttons in the next screen. (See Chapter 10 for more on syncing personal information.)

7. Tap the Save button to finish setting up the account.

tip If you're setting up an iCloud account, this is a good opportunity to enable the Find My iPad feature, which can locate the iPad on a map if you think it's lost or stolen. See Chapter 11 for more detail.

tip If you're still having trouble configuring an account, check out this form from Apple to help you get the right information from your service provider: http://support.apple.com/kb/HT1277.

Read Mail Messages

Before the iPad, I thought the iPhone's implementation of Mail was fine. Not great, but after all, email is mostly just text, right? Now that I've used Mail on the iPad, though, the iPhone version seems like I'm viewing my messages through a keyhole. It works, but the added screen real estate of the iPad makes a huge difference.

Mail presents two different views of your messages, depending on whether you're viewing the iPad in landscape or portrait orientation. The widescreen view displays mailboxes in a pane at left, with the currently selected message at right (**Figure 4.2**). Tap a message to view it.

Figure 4.2
Mail in landscape orientation

Unread message

Active message

Flagged message

The tall view displays only the current message. To browse messages one by one, tap the Previous and Next buttons (**Figure 4.3**). Or, to view and access other messages in the mailbox, tap the button at upper left, which is labeled with the name of the active mailbox. The list of messages slides into view.

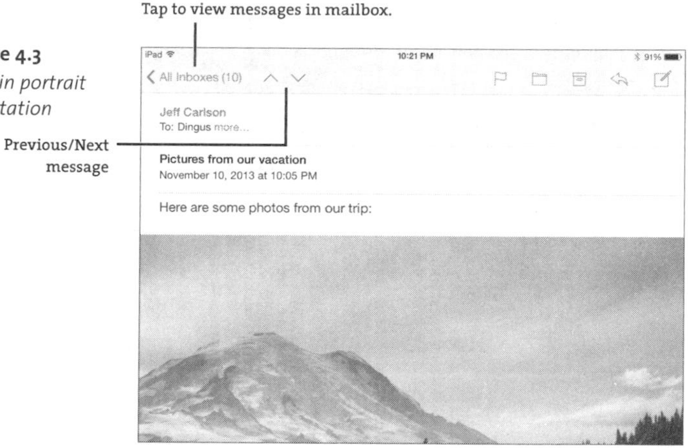

Tap to view messages in mailbox.

Figure 4.3
Mail in portrait orientation

Previous/Next message

tip   Instead of tapping the mailbox name to view the messages list in the portrait view, swipe anywhere using one finger left to right. I use this shortcut all the time.

tip   While reading a message, enlarge the body text by spreading two fingers in the pinch-outward gesture.

tip   Tap the More link in the To field to reveal the From, To, and Cc fields (when addresses appear in them), which are otherwise hidden. You can also make sure they're visible by default; go to Settings > Mail, Contacts, Calendars and set the Show To/Cc Label switch to On.

Check for new mail

When the iPad is connected to the Internet, it can check for new messages, even when Mail isn't the active app, using two methods: Push, where new messages are delivered to Mail as soon as they're available; and Fetch, where Mail contacts each account's server to see if there are any new messages. Of course, you can also perform a manual check whenever you want.

Check mail manually

Opening the Mail app triggers a check for new messages, so that's usually all you need to do. If you're eagerly awaiting a response from someone, you can also use a technique called "pull to refresh." Drag the message list down (**Figure 4.4**). When the icon turns into a spinning progress indicator, you can remove your finger from the surface.

Figure 4.4
Pull to refresh

note   Since the iPad is a mobile device, it's likely you could be checking mail using a cellular network connection or on a Wi-Fi network that doesn't belong to you, like at a coffee shop. If you're concerned about securing the Internet connection, see Chapter 11 to learn how to set up a VPN (virtual private network).

Get new mail using Push

Push is available for iCloud, Exchange, and Yahoo accounts. Do the following to enable it:

1. Go to Settings > Mail, Contacts, Calendars.

2. Tap the Fetch New Data button.

3. Make sure the Push option is set to On.

Generally, Push applies to all of your accounts that support the feature. However, it's possible to disable Push for some accounts: On the same Fetch New Data screen as above, tap an account name, and then choose the Fetch or Manual option instead of Push.

Check mail on a schedule

For accounts that can't use Push, you can specify an interval for when Mail does its check, which happens in the background no matter which app is running and even if the iPad is asleep.

1. Go to Settings > Mail, Contacts, Calendars.

2. Tap the Fetch New Data button.

3. Tap a time interval to select it (**Figure 4.5**). If you choose Manually, the accounts are checked only when you open Mail or tap the Refresh button.

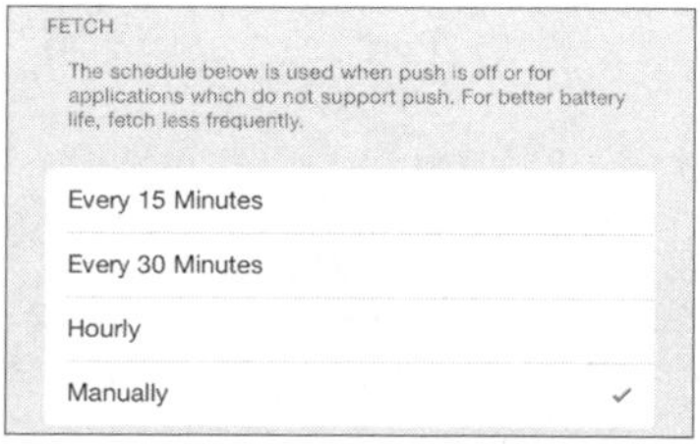

Figure 4.5
Specify how often Mail checks for new messages.

FETCH	
The schedule below is used when push is off or for applications which do not support push. For better battery life, fetch less frequently.	
Every 15 Minutes	
Every 30 Minutes	
Hourly	
Manually	✓

When new mail arrives, the Mail icon on the Home screen appears with a badge indicating the total number of unread messages in all accounts. The mailbox navigation button within Mail also displays an unread message count in the portrait orientation (**Figure 4.6**).

Figure 4.6
New mail indicators

Unread messages

Read email conversations

Email is a time-delayed medium: You could send a message to a friend, who replies several hours later, and then you respond to his message a few minutes after that. Meanwhile, other messages are arriving in your Inbox. Mail helps you keep conversations sensible by grouping them.

Look for a double angle-bracket (>>) symbol to the right of a message's preview (**Figure 4.7**). Tap that message to reveal a list of the messages in that conversation.

Figure 4.7
Viewing an email conversation

A conversation containing multiple messages

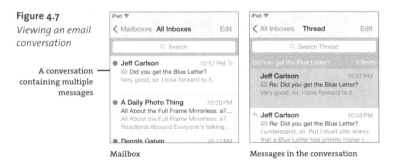

Mailbox

Messages in the conversation

Navigate accounts and mailboxes

It's not unusual for someone to have more than one email account. Mail's unified Inbox displays all incoming messages as if they're in one mailbox. The unified Inbox is the default view, as you can see in Figure 4.7; the title of the message list indicates you're viewing "All Inboxes."

When you do want to dig into specific mailboxes, you can use the controls in the navigation bar that appears either at the top of the left-hand pane (landscape orientation) or at the top of the list slider (portrait orientation). This works for accessing any account's mailboxes, such as Sent Mail, not just the Inbox.

1. Tap the Mailboxes button to view the Mailboxes and Accounts lists (**Figure 4.8**).

2. Tap the name of an account.

3. Tap a mailbox to open it.

4. Tap the message you want to read.

Figure 4.8
Navigating an account hierarchy

Tap Mailboxes button.   Tap mailbox.   Tap message.

> **tip** To preview more of each message in the mailbox list, go to Settings > Mail, Contacts, Calendars; tap the Preview button; and choose up to five visible lines of text.

View file attachments

Although email isn't the most effective delivery mechanism for sending files, people frequently attach documents to messages. Mail on the iPad does a good job of handling most common types of files you're likely to encounter, such as images, PDF files, and Microsoft Word documents, among others.

A file attachment is included in the body of a message (**Figure 4.9**). The appearance of the attachment depends on the file's type and size:

- Images generally appear unaltered, as long as Mail can preview the format.

- Large files are not automatically downloaded, and they appear with a dotted outline and generic download icon.

- A file that Mail cannot display within the message body shows up as an icon containing the file name and size.

Figure 4.9
File attachments

Microsoft Word file ⎯⎯⎯

To preview or open an attachment, do the following:

1. Tap the icon to see a full-screen preview (if Mail can read it), which Apple calls Quick Look.

2. In the preview, tap the Share button in the upper-right corner of the screen. A popover displays which apps can work with the file; tap one to launch the app and open the file. You can also print the attachment from here.

tip If a compatible app is installed, the file attachment icon reflects that app's document format, so it's usually easy to tell right away whether you can open an attachment.

You can also access those options directly without first viewing the Quick Look preview. Touch and hold the icon until a popover appears with options to open in a compatible app or to choose another (**Figure 4.10**).

Figure 4.10
Choose how to view or open the attachment.

Act on special data

As you read your email, Mail recognizes some data types and turns them into links. Tapping a Web address, as you might expect, opens the site in Safari. But Mail can also identify and act on street addresses, phone numbers, and email addresses. Tap an email address, and a new outgoing message is created. Tap a street address, and the Maps app launches and shows you the location.

You can also choose how to interact with the data. Touch and hold a link and then choose an option from the popover that appears (**Figure 4.11**).

Figure 4.11
*Acting on a link
in a message*

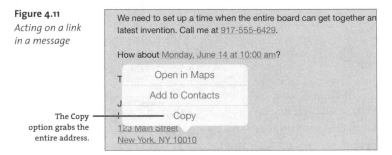

The Copy
option grabs the
entire address.

View information about senders and recipients

In its attempt to shield people from complexity, Apple chose to show email senders and recipients as friendly named blobs instead of addresses like "norville.barnes.hud@gmail.com." Those blobs become useful buttons, however.

Tap any sender or recipient to view more information. If the person is not in your list of contacts, you can easily add them by tapping the Create New Contact button (**Figure 4.12**). The popover changes to let you edit contact information; tap Done to add the person to your Contacts list. Or, tap Add to Existing Contact if this is a different address for someone you already know.

On the other hand, tapping the button of a person already in your Contacts list displays all of their information. That makes it easy to tap their address to view the location in the Maps app, for example.

Figure 4.12
*Viewing sender
information*

App Camp For Girls
To: Jeff Carlson more

Sender

App Camp For Girls

other
jean@appcamp4girls.com

Add the sender to
your Contacts list, or
add the address to
an existing contact. ——

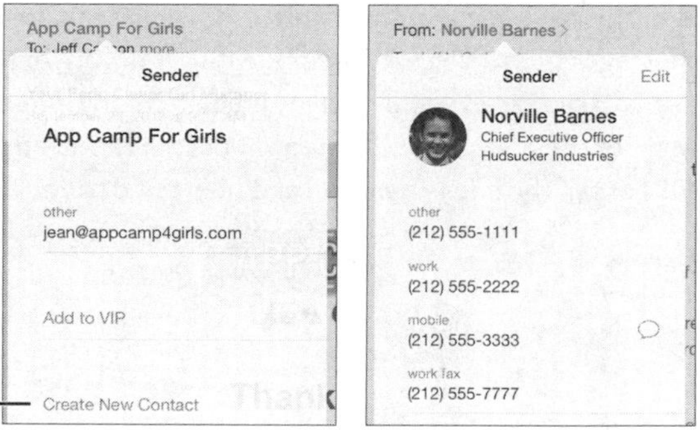

Add to VIP

Create New Contact

A new sender

From: Norville Barnes ›

Sender   Edit

Norville Barnes
Chief Executive Officer
Hudsucker Industries

other
(212) 555-1111

work
(212) 555-2222

mobile
(212) 555-3333

work fax
(212) 555-7777

Someone you already know

> **tip** Viewing information about a sender or recipient also reveals a neat
> shortcut. Say you want to send a friend the contact information of
> someone else you know. Instead of opening the Contacts app, you can do it
> from within Mail. Locate a message from—or addressed to—the person whose
> information you want to share. Tap the person's name. In the popover that
> appears, scroll to the bottom of the information and tap the Share Contact
> button. A new outgoing message is created with the contact's information
> stored in a vCard (.vcf) file as an attachment. When your friend receives the
> email, he can add the vCard file to his contact-management software.

Identify VIPs

Mail's VIP feature helps ensure you don't miss messages from important
people. Any name you've marked as a VIP appears with a star next to it.
(If you use a Mac running OS X 10.8 Mountain Lion or later, you can configure VIPs in the Mail application, too.)

To set someone as a VIP, do the following:

1. Tap a contact's name in the address field of an email message.

2. Tap the Add to VIP button.

What I most like about the feature is the ability to quickly view all messages from a VIP; for example, without having to perform a separate search, I can see everything in my inbox from my wife. Navigate to the Mailboxes list and either tap the VIP button to view messages from all VIPs or tap the info (ⓘ) button and select one of your VIPs (**Figure 4.13**).

Figure 4.13
The VIP mailbox

Tap here to view
a list of all VIPs.

tip At the bottom of the VIP list, tap the VIP Alerts button to jump to the iPad's Notifications settings. You can configure additional attention-grabbers, such as a custom new mail sound, a visual alert style, and whether alerts show up in Notification Center.

Flag messages

Another way to help you differentiate important messages is to flag them. Doing so adds an orange flag to the message and also allows you to view all flagged messages from the Mailboxes list.

In an open message, tap the Flag button and then choose Flag from the popover that appears (**Figure 4.14**). The Flag button is also where you can mark a message as being unread, such as when you want to view it fresh on another device.

Figure 4.14
Flagging a message

Compose Mail Messages

If only we could sit back in lounge chairs, feet propped on a table, and read email all day long like the people in Apple's iPad commercials. Alas, email demands interaction, so at some point you'll find yourself writing new messages and replying to existing ones.

Create a new mail message

In Mail, do the following:

1. Tap the New Message (✐) button. An empty message appears.

2. In the To field, begin typing the name of the person you want to send the email to. Mail displays a list of possible contacts (**Figure 4.15**); tap one to enter it.

   You can also tap the Add (⊕) button to view a popover containing all your contacts; scroll or use the search field to locate a person.

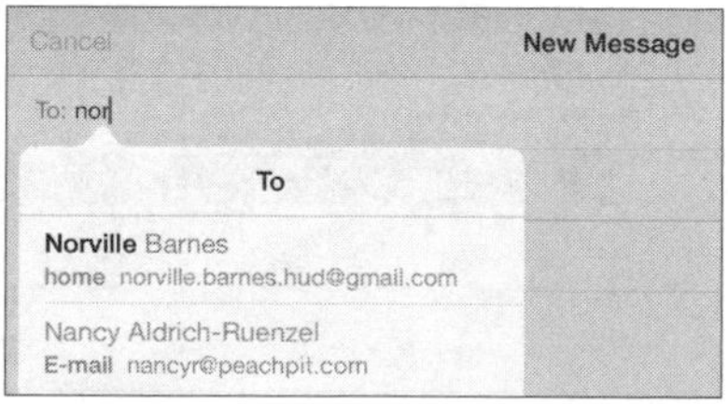

Figure 4.15
List of suggested mail recipients

tip You can type any part of a person's name or email address to find a match; you don't need to always begin with the correct address or the person's first name.

3. If you want to copy other people on the message, tap the Cc/Bcc, From field. Enter addresses into the Cc (carbon copy) or Bcc (blind carbon copy) fields.

    If you prefer to send the message from another account, tap the From field and choose one from the popover that appears.

tip Mail's preferences include an option to specify a default outgoing account (go to Settings > Mail, Contacts, Calendars; tap the Default Account button; and select one of your accounts). However, the setting applies only when you're creating new messages in other apps, such as when you send a link to a Web page in Safari. When you create a new message in Mail, the message is addressed as coming from whichever account you're currently viewing.

4. Tap the Subject field and enter a short title. (Don't leave it blank; many mail servers flag messages with empty Subject lines as spam.)

5. Type or dictate your message into the main field.

6. If you want to add minimal formatting—bold, italic, or underline—select the range of text to alter. In the options bar that appears, tap the Format button and then choose which style to use (**Figure 4.16**).

Figure 4.16
Writing the email message

Format button ——

7. To add a photo or video from the Photos app to the message, touch and hold in the message field for a second to bring up the options bar and choose Insert Photo or Video. You can then pick an image from your library.

   Mail grabs the original photo for you, but if the size is too big for your liking, tap the Cc/Bcc field, which reveals an Image Size field; tap a size (Small, Medium, Large, Actual Size) to compress the image.

8. When you're finished, tap the Send button.

   If you're not ready to dispatch the message, tap the Cancel button and then tap Save Draft to store the email in the Drafts folder for editing and sending later.

note Outgoing messages have the text "Sent from my iPad" appended to the end, a bit of text called a signature. You can change the text in Mail's preferences. Go to Settings > Mail, Contacts, Calendars and tap the Signature button. Edit the text to whatever you like, then apply the change by returning to the Mail, Contacts, Calendars screen.

tip Mail's messages can handle more than just text, as I mentioned when talking about opening file attachments earlier. For outgoing messages, for example, this means you could copy a block of content on a Web page in Safari—with its text formatting and graphics—and paste it into a Mail message.

Reply to a mail message or forward it

When a message requires a response, reply to the sender:

1. With a message open, tap the Reply/Forward (⟲) button.

2. Tap Reply in the popover that appears. A new outgoing message is created, with the contents of the previous message quoted at the bottom of the message area.

3. Type your reply and then tap Send.

tip When you reply to or forward a message, the entire referenced message is quoted. Often it's better to include just one relevant line or paragraph that you're responding to. Before tapping the Reply/Forward button, select the range of text to quote; only that section appears (Figure 4.17). You can also change the quote level if you're quoting something that's gone back and forth in conversation a few times. Touch and hold in a line until the options appear, and tap the Quote Level button; then tap the Decrease or Increase button.

Figure 4.17
Replying with selected text

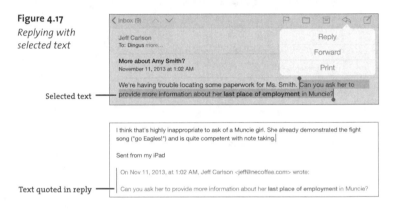

Selected text

Text quoted in reply

note There's no way to attach a file other than a photo or video in an outgoing message within Mail. That doesn't mean attachments aren't possible, though. You just need to do it from whichever app has the content you wish to share via email. For example, in the Pages app you can share a document by email, which creates a new outgoing mail message with the file already attached.

Manage Mail Messages

Though it's not the same as dealing with a foot-high stack of paper letters, I find confronting an Inbox with hundreds of messages a psychic drain. Mail on the iPad doesn't have the same depth of features for managing email that you'll find in a desktop application, but it does let you delete, file, and search for messages.

Delete a message

Unless you're an obsessive archivist, don't try to keep every message. To delete a message after you've read it, tap the Delete (🗑) button in the toolbar. The message is moved to the account's Trash folder. (For some accounts, like Gmail, the Delete button is replaced by an Archive [🗔] button.)

Even better, delete a message without reading it. When you're viewing the contents of a mailbox and see a message that's clearly undesirable (I get a lot of spam, can you tell?), do this: Swipe one finger across the item from right to left; then tap the Trash button (**Figure 4.18**).

Figure 4.18
Swipe to delete.

< Back	**Inbox**	Done

Q Search

9/25/13
ches New Version fo...
are well. I wanted to   More   Trash ——— Tap to delete.
Swipe across. ——— ep Cycle's newest 4...

tip In iOS 6 and earlier, you could swipe in either direction to delete a message, but iOS 7 supports only right-to-left swiping.

Move a message

To keep a message but get it out of the way in your Inbox, file it in another folder within your account.

1. With the message open, tap the Move (🗂) button.

2. Tap a mailbox in the Mailboxes list in the sidebar to move the message there.

Delete or move multiple messages

Sending messages to the Trash or to other mailboxes one by one will make you crazy if there are many to process. Instead, delete or move them in batches.

1. Display the contents of a mailbox, either by tapping its name in the toolbar in portrait orientation or by turning to landscape orientation.

2. Tap the Edit button in the navigation bar.

3. Tap the messages you wish to delete or move. The ones you select gain a checkmark and appear in a stack to the right (**Figure 4.19**).

Figure 4.19
Process multiple messages.

Selected messages —

Mark, Move, and
Trash buttons —

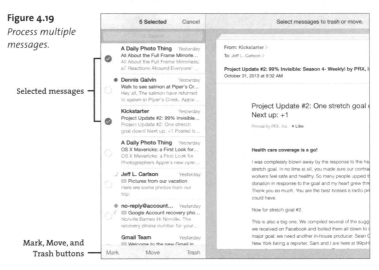

4. Tap the Mark, Move, or Trash button at the lower-left corner of the mailbox. (The Mark button can set the message status as Unread, Flagged, or Junk, for your attention later.) Or, tap the Cancel button at the top if you change your mind.

Search for messages

A powerful tool for managing piles of email is the capability to find something quickly by performing a search.

1. Go to the mailbox you want to search and then tap the search field.

2. Tap a button to specify which portion of the messages should be searched: the From field, the To field, the Subject field, or All.

3. Type a term in the search field. Results appear in the list (**Figure 4.20**).

4. Tap a message to read it.

Figure 4.20
Searching a mailbox

> **tip** Mail defaults to searching through all mailboxes, but you can limit it to just the current one. Pull down on the search results and tap the Current Mailbox button.

Dealing with Email Spam

The Mail app doesn't offer much help with unsolicited junk mail, making the iPad less desirable as one's primary destination for email. You can move a message to the Junk folder by tapping the Flag button, but Mail doesn't filter for spam. Fortunately, most Internet service providers offer spam filtering at the server level, so a lot of the dreck out there gets trapped before it reaches your iPad.

Communicate Using Messages

Cell phone owners have long enjoyed (and abused in quantity) the ability to send and receive SMS texts, which turn out to be enormously expensive relative to the amount of data that's actually being sent. With its Messages app, Apple broke the cellular carriers' chokehold on texts by sending the same data over the Internet for free. The iPad isn't a cell phone, but using the Messages app, you can communicate with other people who own a device running iOS 5.0 or later.

Set up Messages

Messages uses your Apple ID email address to route incoming messages. You can also specify other addresses that people can use to send messages to you. And if you own an iPhone with the same Apple ID, you can receive messages directed to your phone number, too.

1. Go to Settings > Messages and tap the Send & Receive button.

2. Choose one of the addresses iCloud knows about, or tap Add Another Email and enter an email address.

3. In the "Start new conversations from" section, choose the address you want other people to reply to. This setting is important if you want all of your iMessage-capable devices to track the same conversations.

4. Go back to the Messages screen to apply the setting.

> **tip** Siri understands commands such as "Send a text to Kimberly" and "Read the most recent text message" for interacting with Messages, even if you're not currently in the Messages app.

Send a text message

You can send a text to an email address or a phone number (provided the number belongs to someone who also has Messages on their iPhone).

1. In Messages, tap the New Message (⬜) button.

2. Type the name or address of the person to whom you want to communicate in the To field that appears. You can add multiple recipients to create a group message.

3. In the message line just above the keyboard, type or dictate a message (**Figure 4.21**). It's also possible to send photos or videos—tap the camera button to capture a new shot or choose from your photo library.

4. Tap Send.

Conversations appear above the message line in dialog balloons.

Figure 4.21
Sending a text in Messages

tip Touch and hold a dialog balloon to bring up the option to copy its contents, if you want to paste it elsewhere (such as Mail).

tip Want to know when you sent a message? Drag from right to left to expose a timestamp to the right of your messages (Figure 4.22).

Figure 4.22
See when you sent a message.

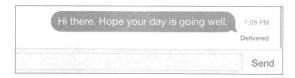

5

Capture Photos and Video

The iPad and iPad mini each include two built-in cameras for capturing photos and video: one mounted on the back and one at the front. After a couple of generations of lackluster hardware, the cameras in the iPad Air and iPad mini are now nice and sharp. The front-facing FaceTime HD camera is great for making FaceTime video calls. The camera on the back captures 5 megapixels of data, features great lens elements, and captures 1080p video with automatic image stabilization. (The cameras on the iPad 2, however, just barely pass muster.)

And yet, specifications quickly lose their importance when you're video-chatting with a friend in another city or capturing a photo or video that you otherwise might have missed. Specs improve over time, but events happen now.

Shoot Photos

Many apps take advantage of the cameras—if you haven't already played with the included Photo Booth app, definitely check it out for a lot of fun—but I'll cover the basics of using the iPad's Camera app.

Capture a photo

You know how camera manufacturers boast that their cameras have large 2.5-inch or 3-inch LCD screens? How about a 7.9-inch or 9.7-inch screen? When you open the Camera app, nearly the entire screen is a preview of what you're about to capture. Here are the basics of getting a shot; I'll go into some of the options shortly.

1. Tap the Camera app to open it. (The first time you use the app, you're asked to give permission to use your location. Go ahead; every photo is tagged with its GPS position.)

2. Select a mode by swiping up or down in the middle of the screen:

   - **Photo:** The default mode uses the entire screen.

   - **Square:** Inspired by Instagram's square format, Apple added a Square option to the Camera app, which crops the edges.

   - **HDR:** Tap the HDR Off button to enable the HDR (High Dynamic Range) mode, which works with either the Photo or Square formats. The iPad captures two images at two different exposures, and then blends them for a better overall exposure (helpful if a subject in the foreground is in dark shadows, for example). The original and the HDR version are both saved.

note If you find yourself taking photos often with the iPad, you'll soon want more than what the built-in Camera app offers. Check out the app Camera+ (campl.us) for advanced features like setting separate focus and white balance points.

3. Compose your shot using the preview on the screen (**Figure 5.1**); the iPad senses whether it's in portrait or landscape orientation.

To toggle between the rear and front cameras, tap the Camera Switch button.

If you see one or more yellow boxes appear, the Camera app is identifying what it thinks is a person's face. When you take the shot, it uses that area as the focus point.

Figure 5.1
The Camera app interface

Switch cameras

Shutter button   Switch modes

4. Press the shutter button to take a shot.

The photo is saved in the iPad's Camera Roll, which is accessible by tapping the preview button in the lower-right corner of the screen or by opening the Photos app. (See Chapter 6 for more on viewing photos.)

tip If you press and hold the shutter button, the iPad starts capturing images (about two per second) until you lift your finger.

Choose a focus point, exposure, and white balance

The camera usually focuses on the center of the screen, but you can specify any area on which to focus. Tap once to set the focus point, which is represented by a yellow square (**Figure 5.2**).

The iPad also uses that focus area as the basis to set exposure and white balance. So, for example, if a person in the foreground is silhouetted by a bright background, touch and hold the person to lighten the foreground. You'll see AE/AF Lock appear at the top of the screen, which indicates that the exposure and focus are both locked.

Figure 5.2
Specifying focus

Zoom in on a subject

Is the thing you want to photograph a bit too far away? Using the Camera app's digital zoom feature, you can enlarge the image up to five times.

1. Pinch outward with two fingers, just as you would to zoom in on a photo or Web page. A zoom slider appears at the bottom of the screen.

2. While the slider is visible, you can drag it for more precise zooming. Or, touch and hold the + and − buttons at each end (**Figure 5.3**).

Figure 5.3
*Zoom in to
get closer.*

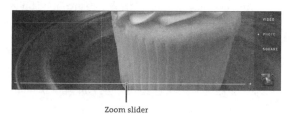

Zoom slider

note   Expect the image to degrade when you use the digital zoom feature. Unlike optical zoom, where a telephoto lens moves to enlarge the image, digital zoom accomplishes the resizing solely in software. The processor is making a best-guess estimate of what the image looks like blown up, so the result may be softer than you'd prefer.

Capture Video

Shooting video is similar to capturing still photos.

1. In the Camera app, switch to the video mode.

2. Optionally, choose which camera to use by tapping the Camera Switch button.

3. Tap the Record button (which now includes a red recording indicator instead of a camera icon) to start recording.

4. Tap the Record button again to stop. As with photos, the video you shoot is added to the Camera Roll.

note   Under iOS 7, you can tap the screen to set or lock focus and exposure in the Video mode, and also use digital zoom (which wasn't available in earlier versions). Those controls apply after you've begun recording, too.

Make FaceTime Calls

Videoconferencing on computers has been around for years—iChat, Skype, and Google Hangouts are just a few options. But as I've learned recently, a toddler's desire to sit in front of a computer screen, even when talking to grandparents, is short-lived. FaceTime on the iPad brings video chatting to wherever you are, and the ability to switch cameras lets you follow your subject around or point to something you want to feature (like the child's latest dance moves).

Set up your FaceTime account

FaceTime uses your Apple ID to identify itself on the network, so other people using FaceTime can connect with you. If you didn't specify this information when you set up the iPad, here's how to configure FaceTime.

1. Open the Settings app and select FaceTime in the left column.

2. Enter your Apple ID and password.

3. Tap the Sign In button.

Once you've entered your Apple ID, you can assign other email addresses (for example, if you don't want to give out your Apple ID to others). In the FaceTime settings, tap the Add Another Email button and enter a valid email address. With multiple addresses available, a new Caller ID field appears, which is the address that appears in a friend's copy of FaceTime when you call them. Tap it to choose from your list of addresses.

Set up a FaceTime contact

1. Tap the FaceTime app to open it.

2. Tap the Contacts button to view the people in your Contacts list. If you're just starting out, the list may be empty. Otherwise, if you

synced contacts from your computer, they should appear here. I'm assuming here you're starting from scratch; if not, skip ahead to "Make a FaceTime call."

3. Tap the + button to create a new contact.

4. Enter the person's first and last name, phone number (if you know it), and email address (again, if you know it) (**Figure 5.4**).

Figure 5.4
Creating a new FaceTime contact

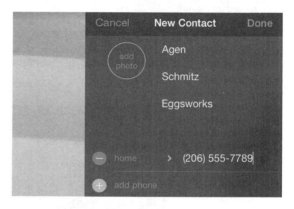

If the person owns an iPhone 4 or later, they're capable of chatting via FaceTime using their mobile number. Other owners of camera-equipped iPads, or friends who have the FaceTime application installed on their Macs, are identified by their email addresses.

5. Tap Done to finish setting up the contact.

note If you're planning to travel outside your home country, FaceTime needs to know where you are so it can properly dial contacts whose FaceTime devices are accessible via phone number. In the FaceTime settings, tap your Account button, and then tap the Change Location button that appears. Lastly, tap Region and choose a country from the list. Tap the Save button to finish.

Make a FaceTime call

1. Tap the Contacts button to view your list of contacts.

2. Tap the name of the person you want to chat with.

3. Tap the person's phone number or email address to initiate a call.

4. When the other person accepts the FaceTime request, you're connected (**Figure 5.5**).

Figure 5.5
A FaceTime video chat

The small window in the corner displays what your camera is sending so you can make sure your face is in the frame. If you wish to move it to another corner, drag it there.

5. To switch between the iPad's two cameras, tap the button at the left in the control bar. You can also mute the audio of your side of the conversation by tapping the Mute button at right.

6. When you're finished with the call, tap the End button to disconnect.

tip FaceTime isn't just for video! As long as both participants are using the app, you can have audio-only calls (which boast great sound quality).

tip Tapping the Mute button only silences the audio; it does not pause the video image. If you want to mute the audio and also pause the image, first tap the Mute button and then press the iPad's Home button to switch to the Home screen. The FaceTime call is still active—you can see a status indicator in the menubar (**Figure 5.6**)—but your image is frozen to the other person. (If you just exit FaceTime without first tapping the Mute button, you can still talk to the person at the other end of the connection.) Tap the green indicator to return to FaceTime.

Figure 5.6
A green status bar indicates a FaceTime call is active.

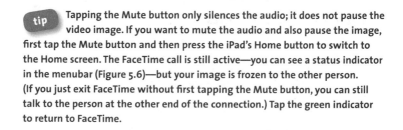

View recent calls

FaceTime keeps track of previous calls and attempted calls. Tap the Recents button to view them. You can also use this area to add an incoming caller to your list of contacts. Tap the info () button next to a person's name to view details about the call (**Figure 5.7**). Then tap either the Create New Contact button or the Add to Existing Contact button.

Figure 5.7
A recent call log

Add a contact to the Favorites list

Rather than search through your contacts for people you frequently call, add them to the Favorites list, accessible by tapping the Favorites button.

1. In the Contacts list, tap the name of a person to view their details.

2. Tap the Add to Favorites button.

3. If there are multiple contact possibilities, such as a mix of phone numbers and email addresses, choose one from the popover that appears.

Or, do the following:

1. Tap the Favorites button to view your Favorites list.

2. Tap the Add (+) button and select a person in your Contacts list.

3. Choose the phone number or email address the person uses for FaceTime. If you've previously participated in a FaceTime chat with them, a blue camera icon appears next to the item.

The person then appears in the Favorites list.

tip   FaceTime can block video and audio requests from callers you choose. Open the Recents list, tap the info button for the person you wish to block, and then tap the Block This Caller button at the bottom of the contact information. Blocked callers are found in Settings > FaceTime if you want to take someone out of the penalty box later.

note   On cellular-capable iPads, you can choose whether FaceTime works over the cellular connection. Open Settings > Cellular Data, find FaceTime in the list of apps, and set the switch to On. Doing so lets you use FaceTime anywhere you have a connection. (But expect it to burn through bandwidth, and depending on your carrier, additional fees might apply.)

View Photos

Just *look* at that screen! Full color, larger than a phone, Retina resolution, attached to a device that's more comfortable to hold than a laptop. If the iPad didn't already do a thousand other things, you'd think it was designed solely for displaying digital photos.

When you have an iPad stocked with your favorite photos, you have a portable presentation machine. Maybe you want to show off your latest snapshots. Maybe you're a photographer (or real estate agent, or designer, or...) showing a portfolio to a prospective client. Maybe you want to store photos on the iPad while on vacation instead of toting a laptop. Maybe you need to display a slideshow using a projector or an HDTV. Or maybe you just want to be able to look at your favorite photos whenever you feel like it. The Photos app can deliver your images.

Getting Photos onto the iPad

Where are your photos coming from? You have four options: sync photos from your computer; import photos directly from a camera or memory card; send photos to an email account you check on the iPad; or copy pictures from Web pages in Safari.

Sync photos from the computer

With most photos now being captured digitally, it's likely you use photo management software to keep track of them all. Or, you might prefer to organize the image files in a folder on disk. iTunes can handle both.

Sync with photo management software

iTunes recognizes libraries in iPhoto 4.0.3 or later and Aperture 3.0.2 or later on the Mac, and Photoshop Elements 3.0 or later for Windows.

1. Connect the iPad to the computer, open iTunes, and select the iPad.

2. Click the Photos tab.

3. Enable the Sync Photos From option and choose your photo software from the pop-up menu (**Figure 6.1**).

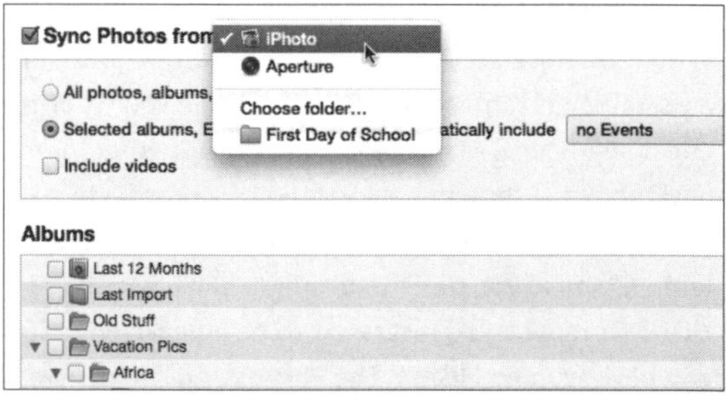

Figure 6.1
*Photos pane
in iTunes*

4. To transfer your entire library, choose the first option: All photos, albums, events, and faces.

Or, enable the second radio button and then mark the checkboxes of any albums, events (or projects, in Aperture), or faces.

Using the radio button's pop-up menu, you can make some items appear automatically. For example, regardless of which checkboxes are selected in the Events or Projects list, you can choose to have the photos from all events from the last month appear on the iPad.

note The option to group photos based on events/projects or faces is supported only if you're syncing with iPhoto or Aperture. If you're using Photoshop Elements in Windows, you get the option of syncing all photos and albums or specifying selected albums.

5. To copy video files located in your library, select the Include Videos checkbox.

6. Click the Sync button. iTunes transfers the photos to the iPad.

tip The information in this chapter really only touches on what's possible with photos on the iPad. In fact, I wrote an entire book about the subject: *The iPad for Photographers*, now in its second edition, available from Peachpit Press and your favorite bookstore. See ipadforphotographers.com for more information.

Sync with a folder

Some people prefer to manage image files manually or use software—such as Adobe Photoshop Elements—that organizes and displays photos in folders. iTunes can use the folder contents, including subfolders, as the media source for the Photos app.

1. In the Photos pane, choose the Pictures (Mac) or My Pictures (Windows) default locations. Or, click Choose Folder and specify a different folder.

2. To include everything in the folder, choose the All Folders option. Or, click the Selected Folders button and mark the checkboxes for the folders you wish to sync in the Folders list (**Figure 6.2**).

Figure 6.2
Sync photos from subfolders.

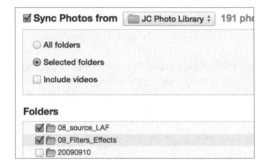

3. Click the Apply button to start the transfer.

> **tip** The iTunes interface is a little confusing on this part. In the previous example, the only photos transferred are the ones in folders that are selected. What's not synced are the photos in the parent folder, "JC Photo Library." If I wanted just the images in that folder, and none of the images from the subfolders, I'm out of luck: I'd get either the contents of specific subfolders (Selected Folders option) or everything in "JC Photo Library," subfolders included (All Folders option). So, if you're going to organize photos at the folder level, I recommend storing image files in subfolders, not parent folders.

Import photos from a camera

Using Apple's optional iPad camera adapters, you don't need iTunes as a middleman. The iPad Camera Connection kit includes two adapters that connect to the 30-pin dock connector on third-generation iPads and earlier: one that accepts SD memory cards and one that accepts a standard USB cable. For the iPad Air, iPad mini, and fourth-generation Retina iPad, you can buy separate adapters that plug into the Lightning port.

tip Wait, did I just say that the iPad can gain a regular USB port? Yes...but there are strings attached. The iPad uses the USB camera connector for transferring image and video files only—but there are a couple of surprises, too. Plug in a USB headset to listen to audio or use a headset's microphone. The benefit of this approach over plugging iPhone-compatible headphones into the iPad's headphone port is the ability to use higher-quality audio electronics. For example, I own a Sennheiser headset that's normally connected to my Mac for Skype calls; I can do the same (using the Skype app) on my iPad now. The other surprise is that the connector recognizes some USB keyboards, which is great if you don't own the iPad Keyboard Dock or a Bluetooth wireless keyboard. (You may need to connect devices through a powered USB hub for them to work.)

To import photos via a camera adapter, do the following:

1. Plug one of the adapters into the iPad.

2. Insert an SD card or plug in a USB cable connected to your camera, depending on which adapter you're using. If the latter, turn on the camera's power.

tip You can even transfer photos directly from an iPhone: Connect the iPhone's sync cable to the USB connector. (Unfortunately, the iPad can't charge the iPhone's battery over this connection, which would be cool.)

3. Wake the iPad and open the Photos app (if it doesn't open automatically).

4. Tap the Import button.

5. To import everything, tap the Import All button. The images begin to copy to the iPad. Skip ahead to Step 7.

6. If you'd rather import just some of the images, tap the ones you want; a blue checkmark indicates the ones you've selected (**Figure 6.3**).

Figure 6.3
Selecting photos for import

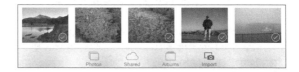

Tap the Import button, which brings up a popover with options to Import All (overriding your selections, in case you changed your mind at the last minute) or Import Selected. Tap one to begin copying the images to the iPad.

Tap the Stop Import button if you want to halt the transfer; doing so doesn't remove any selections you made before importing.

7. When importing is complete, you're given the option to delete or keep the images on the camera or SD card. I advise tapping Keep, and then erasing the card later using the camera's format controls.

8. Remove the SD card or turn off the camera. The transferred photos appear in a new album called Last Import.

tip   Photos imported directly from a camera or card can be deleted later by viewing the image and tapping the Trash button (🗑). To turn the picture 90 degrees counterclockwise, if necessary, tap the Edit button and then the Rotate button.

Import photos from email

Do you have a family member who likes to send photos via email? Rather than digging through your old messages to view those photos later, add them to the iPad's photo collection.

1. In the Mail app, open the message containing the photo attachments.

2. Touch and hold a photo to bring up a share sheet containing actions you can take (**Figure 6.4**).

3. Tap the Save Image button. Or, if several images are included, tap the Save *[number]* Images button. The photos are added to the Camera Roll album in the Photos app.

Figure 6.4
*Saving images
from Mail*

Import photos from other apps

The ability to save images from Mail also applies to other apps. In Safari, for example, touch and hold any image and then tap Save Image to store it. However, keep in mind that images on the Web don't have the same high resolution as ones you'd import from your digital camera, so they may not look as good when expanded to fill the iPad's screen.

View Photos

I've covered the ways to get photos onto the iPad, but that's just preamble for viewing them. iOS 7 adopts a slightly different method of browsing your photo library than earlier versions, offering a handful of views to help you find your images.

View a photo

Open the Photos app and tap the Photos button at the bottom of the screen (if it's not already selected) to see thumbnails of photos stored on the iPad. The app has four viewing levels, each one "zooming in" according to the dates the photos were captured. You'll likely start in the Moments view, but let's take a look at them from the top down:

- **Years.** This beautiful abstract mosaic displays small thumbnails of images grouped by year (**Figure 6.5**).

- **Collections.** This view groups photos by days (or in groups spanning several days, depending on the number of images).

Figure 6.5

The Years and Collections views

tip In the Years and Collections views, drag your finger across the image thumbnails to see a preview. When you lift your finger, the last-previewed image opens in the Photo view.

- **Moments.** The Moments view offers fairly large thumbnails grouped by day.

- **Photo.** Tap any thumbnail to view the photo fullscreen. Rotate the iPad to match the photo's orientation for the best effect (**Figure 6.6**).

Figure 6.6
A photo viewed widescreen

While viewing an image, you can do a number of things:

- Tap once anywhere to make the controls disappear. Tap again to make them reappear.

- Double-tap anywhere on the photo to zoom in. Double-tapping again zooms back out to fit.

- To zoom with more control, pinch two fingers outward. Swipe anywhere on the image to view a different area of the photo. To zoom back out, pinch two fingers together or double-tap the screen.

- To quickly skim all of the photos in the Moments view, tap once to view the controls and then drag the navigation bar at the bottom of the screen (**Figure 6.7**). The preview is extremely fast because the app displays low-resolution images as you drag, giving you a sense of what the photo is without having to draw all of the detail. If you pause, the higher-resolution version appears.

Figure 6.7
Quickly navigating photos

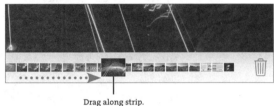

Drag along strip.

View photos in locations

If any of your photos include location tags—GPS coordinates marking where the photos were shot, either written to the file when captured or applied in iPhoto, Aperture, Photoshop Elements, or other software—you can view them on a map. In any of the Photos views, look for a location name above the thumbnails (**Figure 6.8**). (When location data is present, the date gets shifted to the right side of the screen.)

Figure 6.8
Locations appear above thumbnails.

Tap the location name to view a map that features thumbnails marking where photos were taken (**Figure 6.9**). Tap a group of thumbnails to view its photos.

Figure 6.9
*Photos with
location
information*

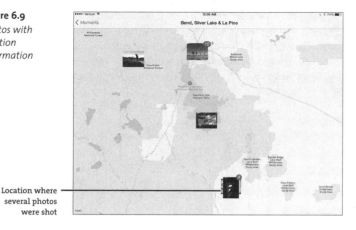

Location where
several photos
were shot

View photos in albums

In addition to the big free-for-all that is the Photos pane, your images are
also organized into albums. Some albums are automatically created by
the iPad: It groups videos and panoramas into their own albums for quick
access, and also collects imported media into Last Import, All Imported,
and Imported Photos & Videos albums. Other albums are those you synced
from a computer. This view is also where you'll find Events and Faces if you
synced them from iPhoto or Aperture. Tap an album to open it.

 I'm a big fan of useless shortcuts—things that were implemented just
because they could be—and here's a great one. Instead of just tapping
a thumbnail to view the photo full screen, use the expanding pinch gesture to
enlarge it. Now, before you let go, *rotate your fingers*. The image can be freely
rotated and scaled as long as your fingers are touching the glass. Why? I couldn't
tell you. Maybe to preview a landscape photo in portrait orientation without
rotating the iPad. Or maybe because the graphics capabilities inside the iPad can
do it, and that's a good enough reason. I don't know, but it's fun to play with.

tip Pinch outward with two fingers on an album to quickly preview what you're about to open. As you do so, the photos within unstack themselves (Figure 6.10). If it's not the set you were expecting, just pinch your fingers together to return the album to its stacked state. When you've expanded a collection far enough, it takes over the entire screen. Tap a photo thumbnail to view the image.

Figure 6.10
Previewing an album

Before

Pinched outward

tip Instead of trying to tap the back button in the upper-left corner of the screen (which is labeled with the name of the enclosing album), pinch two fingers together to collapse the album you're currently viewing. It's much faster, because your fingers are likely already in place from opening a stack or zooming in on an image.

Add photos to albums

The Photos app organizes pictures in several different ways, but you may want to impose your own organization by moving photos to albums.

To create a new empty album, do the following:

1. Go to the Albums pane, tap the Add (+) button, enter a title, and tap Save.

2. Locate the photos you want to add and tap to select them. You can add all photos in a Moment by tapping the Select button at the right side of the screen (**Figure 6.11**).

Figure 6.11
Adding photos to a new album

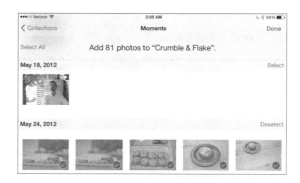

3. Tap Done to add the photos to the new album.

To add photos to an existing album, do the following:

1. When viewing photos in the Moments view or within an album, tap the Select button in the upper-right corner.

2. Select the photos you want to add by tapping them.

3. Tap the Add To button.

4. Select an existing album or tap the New Album button (and enter a name). The photos appear in the album.

> **tip** When you're viewing an album, you can tap the Select button and choose photos to remove. However, note that tapping the Trash (🗑) button only pulls the images out of the album; it doesn't delete them from the iPad's memory.

Edit photos

The Photos app offers a few basic editing features for quick adjustments.

1. With a photo open, tap the Edit button.

2. Do any of the following:

   ■ Tap the Rotate button to turn the image counterclockwise in 90-degree increments. This is useful when a photo's correct orientation wasn't picked up during import.

   ■ Tap the Enhance button to let the Photos app adjust exposure and color as it sees fit.

   ■ Tap the Filters button to apply a distinctive look to the image. (The original is always saved, so you can go back if you decide the filter isn't what you want.)

   ■ If someone in the photo suffers from red-eye, tap the Red-Eye button and then tap the affected eyes.

   ■ To adjust the visible area of the photo, tap the Crop button and drag a corner handle or edge; drag the center of the crop area to reposition it. After you resize the crop area, tap the Constrain button to choose an aspect ratio to enforce. If the photo needs straightening, use two fingers to zoom and then rotate as needed. Tap the Crop button to make the change stick.

3. When you're done making edits, tap the Save button. The app saves the edited version of the photo. (Previous versions of iOS required that you save a new copy of the image, but iOS 7 smartly keeps track of the edited and original copies of the shot.)

Even after you've edited a photo, the Photos app remembers the original. So you can always open the edited version, tap the Edit button, and then tap the Revert to Original button.

tip Want more editing capability? A lot more? Apple's iPhoto for iOS is an impressive app for making detailed adjustments without leaving the iPad. It's available free from the App Store with the purchase of an iPad.

Play a video

Most digital cameras now shoot video as well as stills, so the Photos app can play video, too. In iTunes, make sure you enable the Include Videos option in the Photos pane. The iPad camera adapters also allow you to import videos you've shot directly into the iPad. Some cameras' video may not play, though. When you come across a video clip in the Photos app, do any of the following:

- Tap the Play button that appears in the middle of the screen to start playing. Or, you can tap the Play button in the toolbar (**Figure 6.12**).

- Touch and hold the playhead to skim through the filmstrip and locate a particular section of the video. If you hold for a moment, the filmstrip spreads out horizontally to give you finer control while skimming.

- While the video is playing, tap the Pause button (**||**) to stop playback.

Figure 6.12
Viewing video clips

Video clip thumbnail in the Photos app

Filmstrip

Play/Pause button in toolbar

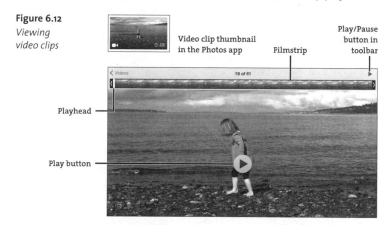

Playhead

Play button

tip Here's a cool side effect of playing videos in the Photos app. Using one of the camera adapters, you can import movies—the Hollywood kind—and watch them on the iPad. For example, if you're going on vacation and you don't want to bring a laptop, but the number of movies you want to watch won't fit on the iPad's internal storage, load up on some inexpensive SD memory cards. Using a program such as HandBrake (www.handbrake.fr) on your computer, digitize your DVDs to digital M4V files. Copy those to one or more SD memory cards, then insert one into the memory card adapter. Transfer a movie to the iPad in the Photos app and then watch it there. (It won't show up in the Videos app.) When you're done, delete the movie and transfer another one. However, there's a catch: The video file must be named something similar to what a digital camera would use. The Photos app won't recognize a file named "Star Wars.MP4", but it will play "IMG_1138.MP4".

tip Another way to beat the limitation of the iPad's internal storage—especially if you bought the 16 GB model and are bumping up against its limit—is to buy an external wireless hard disk, such as the Seagate Wireless Plus. It acts as a portable wireless server, enabling you to stream photos or movies over Wi-Fi. It's great for a long vacation involving lots of movies.

Use iCloud Photo Stream

When the Photo Stream feature of iCloud is enabled, images you capture using the iPad (or an iPhone or iPod touch) appear in the Photos app. Enable the My Photo Stream option in Settings > iCloud > Photos. To view your streams in the Photos app, tap the Albums button at the bottom of the screen and then tap the My Photo Stream album.

Photo Stream automatically keeps 1000 photos on the iPad, including the last 30 days' worth of new photos. If you run across a photo you want to keep on the iPad (before it's rotated out by new photos), add it to the Camera Roll or to an album, as follows:

1. Go to the My Photo Stream album to view your stream.

2. Tap the Select button.

3. Select the photo or photos you wish to keep.

4. Tap the Add To button.

5. Tap the album you want to use (**Figure 6.13**). Or, tap the New Album button, type a name for the album, and tap Save.

Figure 6.13
*Copying Photo
Stream photos
to an album*

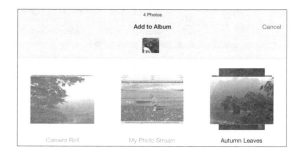

Similarly, you can delete photos from your Photo Stream. With one or more photos selected, as in the steps above, tap the Trash (🗑) button. Tap the Delete *[number of]* Photos button that appears to confirm that you want to remove the images from all devices that share your Photo Stream.

> **tip** Apple no longer restricts the number of photos you can store in your Photo Stream on the iCloud servers, but it does limit the number of uploads and shared images. See http://support.apple.com/kb/HT4858.

Share a Photo Stream

The limitation of the Photo Stream is that it's basically just for your own entertainment—the photos show up on all of your devices, but not on anyone else's.

To share photos from your stream with others, create Shared Photo Streams that appear on their devices or on the Web.

1. In the Photos app, navigate to the Photos or Albums screens and tap the Select button.

2. Tap to select the photos you want to share.

3. Tap the Share button (📤) and then tap the iCloud button.

4. If this is the first shared stream you've created, give the stream a name and tap Next. If not, skip to step 7.

5. Type the names of people you want to share the photos with in the To field, or tap the Add (+) button and choose from your list of contacts. Note that you don't need to include anyone to create a Shared Photo Stream—you can leave this field blank (in case you want to add people later, for example).

6. Tap the Next button.

7. If you've already set up streams, tap the Stream button to choose which stream will receive the images (**Figure 6.14**).

Figure 6.14
Choose a stream and make a comment.

tip In the Moments view, you can also tap the Share button to the right of a Moment's name or location to share all photos or selected ones from that group.

8. Optionally enter a comment that people will see in the email that's sent. The comment must be under 200 characters, although the field doesn't offer a character count the way it does when sharing something to Twitter. And, oddly, the comment is attached to the last photo you added to the set.

9. Tap the Post button to publish the stream. It appears in the Shared screen of the Photos app, which has two views: Shared Streams, which lets you browse them like albums, and Activity, which displays the most recent additions.

Add photos to a Shared Photo Stream

If you want to add photos to a stream later, follow steps 1–3 and then choose a stream in step 7. You don't need to send a new message; the images automatically show up on your friends' devices.

Like and comment on a Shared Photo Stream

You and your friends can "like" and make comments on photos for everyone to see. Tap the Comment button in the lower-left corner of the screen to view comments. Tap the Like button to express your approval, or start typing to compose a comment and then tap Post.

Add subscribers to a Shared Photo Stream

To share a stream with other people, delete a stream, or change its name or public status, go to the Shared pane, tap the stream you want to edit, and tap the People button. This is also where you can allow subscribers to post their own photos to the stream, publish it as a public Web site that anyone can view, and receive notifications when there's activity on the stream.

View a Slideshow

Swiping is fine for showing off a few pictures, but there will be times when you want the iPad to drive a photo presentation. In that case, set up an impromptu slideshow of one of your albums.

1. Open an album or a Shared Photo Stream.

2. Tap the Slideshow button. The Slideshow Options popover appears (**Figure 6.15**).

Figure 6.15
Slideshow options

3. Tap the Transitions button and choose a transition style to use.

4. If you want music to play during the slideshow, set the Play Music switch to On. If not, make sure the option is off and skip the next step.

5. Tap the Music button to choose which music to use. The popover becomes a compact version of the music list in the Music app, where you can navigate your music library by song title, artist, album, playlist, and other criteria.

6. Tap the Start Slideshow button. If you need to cancel the slideshow while it's playing, tap once anywhere on the screen.

The slideshow plays until all photos have been displayed or until the music ends. However, you can customize a few of the slideshow parameters. Go to Settings > Photos & Camera, where you can specify how long each slide appears onscreen (in increments from 2 to 20 seconds), whether the photos (and music) repeat after they've initially appeared, and whether the order should be shuffled. These settings apply to any slideshow you run in the Photos app.

note　Surprisingly, the Photos app lets you play *only one song* during a slideshow—not a playlist, not an album, just one song. Even more mind-bending is that this behavior has never changed, even through several major releases of iOS.

Share Photos

On more than one occasion I've shown a photo to someone who then said, "Ooh, can you send that to me?" Why yes, I certainly can, and it's easy to do. The Photos app features several methods of getting photos off the device: Mail, Message, Twitter, Facebook, Flickr, and AirDrop.

Share one or more photos

To attach a photo to an outgoing message or upload, do the following:

1. Open a photo and tap the Share button ( ).

2. Choose which photos to share by tapping them (a blue checkmark appears on selected shots).

3. Tap the button for the service you want.

4. Depending on the service, add a recipient, a subject, and optional message text.

5. Tap the Send or Post button to dispatch the photo.

tip Many photo sharing services, like Flickr (www.flickr.com), also accept uploads via email. You're given a personal Flickr email address, and any image files sent to that address are posted to your photo stream.

note Although sending files via email is convenient, I don't recommend ganging up a bunch of images together in one message. That increases the chance that a mail server might think you're sending spam or viruses; or your recipient may not have the bandwidth to deal with such large messages.

Print a photo

If you're connected wirelessly to a supported printer, choose Print from the Share screen to print a copy of the photo(s). (See Chapter 1 for more on printing.)

Copy a photo

To copy the image to the iPad's temporary memory, choose Copy from the Share popover. When viewing a collection, you can also touch and hold a photo thumbnail and choose Copy. After copying the photo, you can paste it elsewhere, such as in another app or in an email message.

Assign a photo to a contact

If you have a photo of a friend whose information is in your Contacts app, choose the Assign to Contact option from the Share screen. Select the person's name in the Contacts list that appears, then pinch and drag to position the photo in the frame. Tap the Use button to assign the photo.

Use a photo as wallpaper

Chapter 2 covers how to set wallpapers in the iPad's Settings app, but in Photos you can do it directly. Choose Use as Wallpaper from the Share popover, then choose Set Lock Screen, Set Home Screen, or Set Both.

View photos on a TV or projector

For a real big-screen slideshow experience, display your photos on an HDTV or a digital projector. The iPad offers two ways to do it: sharing via AirPlay, or connected by special video cables.

Using AirPlay

If you own an Apple TV or other AirPlay-enabled video device, you can send photos to your television wirelessly.

1. Open a photo and tap the Share button (⬆).

2. Tap the AirPlay button.

3. Tap the name of the AirPlay device (**Figure 6.16**). The AirPlay button turns blue to indicate it's active, and your photo appears on the television.

Figure 6.16
Choosing an AirPlay device

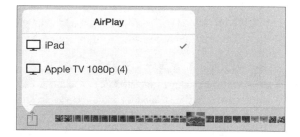

Using a video cable

A number of adapters and cables enable you to connect the iPad to a television. Apple sells Lightning and 30-pin adapters for connecting the iPad via HDMI and VGA, and 30-pin adapters for connecting via component and composite plugs.

Sync imported photos and videos back to the computer

You probably don't intend to keep photos you imported using the iPad camera adapters in the iPad's memory. When you get back to your computer, do the following to move them to its hard drive:

1. Connect the iPad to the computer.

2. Open your photo management software.

3. Use the software's feature for importing photos, just as if you'd attached a camera.

    The computer sees the iPad as a USB storage device. Under Windows, you can view it as you would view an attached disk. On the Mac, you need to use the photo software or the Image Capture application to access the iPad's pictures.

4. After importing the files, delete them from the iPad: Open a collection, tap the Select button, tap to select the images you want to remove, and then tap the Trash button. Tap the Delete *[number of]* Photos button that appears (to confirm your action).

> **tip** There's no good way to select all photos (or even a range of photos) without tapping each individual one, with one exception. In the Moments screen, tap Select, and then you can tap Select for an entire Moment.

> **tip** Some apps transfer photos to the computer wirelessly. I used PhotoSync (www.photosync-app.com) as the main method of moving screenshots from my iPads to my computer while working on this book, for example. Photosmith (www.photosmithapp.com) lets you rate and apply metadata to photos and then import them directly into Adobe Photoshop Lightroom with that information intact.

7

Read Books and Magazines

Under other circumstances, the subject of reading electronic books on a device would warrant a few paragraphs or maybe an extended sidebar. But the iPad's handheld form factor—especially the iPad mini, which is thin and lightweight—and large storage capacity make it an attractive ebook reader. It wouldn't surprise me if some people view the iPad primarily as an ebook reader that also happens to do other stuff.

Instead of packing a tote bag bursting with hardcovers on your next vacation, Apple's iBooks app offers an attractive alternative: Store digital versions of books on the iPad, and connect to the iBooks Store to buy new ones when you need more. And ebooks aren't just plain text anymore—the iBooks Store offers illustrated works, including children's picture books and fine arts books, as well as titles with embedded video.

In addition to purchased books, the iBooks app can also store Adobe Acrobat PDF files, enabling you to read titles from the wide swath of publishers who don't publish in the EPUB format that iBooks uses.

Although this chapter focuses on the features of the iBooks app, that's not the only player out there. If you prefer to buy ebooks from Amazon, the free Kindle app reads titles from the online retailer; and if you previously owned a physical Kindle e-reader, you can keep your existing library.

The iPad can also handle other types of electronic text, with a multitude of media companies offering digital versions of magazines and newspapers, most accessed in standalone apps or viewed in Safari.

Install the iBooks App

The iBooks app isn't included on the iPad by default, but on a new device you'll be prompted to download it and a few other free apps, such as Find My Friends. If you skipped past that step, you can download and install the app by searching for "iBooks" in iTunes or using the App Store on the iPad.

note The iBooks app is available to all international markets that have an App Store. However, the content available in the iBooks Store varies from country to country.

Get Books from the iBooks Store

If this is your first experience with ebooks, iBooks will be empty. However—and this will come as a surprise—Apple is ready and eager to sell electronic books to you in its iBooks Store. The store is available only from within the iBooks app, but it uses your iTunes Store account.

To access the iBooks Store, tap the Store button. Browsing is similar to shopping at the iTunes Store.

- If you want to download a free book to get started without buying anything, scroll to the bottom of the Featured page and tap Free Books.

- Tap a book title to view more information about it (**Figure 7.1**).

Figure 7.1
*Viewing info
about a book*

- To purchase the book, tap the price button, which changes to read "Buy Book." Tap the button again to buy the book, which, after you enter your account and password, downloads to your library.

- Tap the Sample button to download a sample (usually the first chapter or a sizable excerpt). It appears in your library with a Sample banner on the cover (**Figure 7.2**). If you like the book, tap the Buy button that appears at the top of the screen or at the end of the sample.

Figure 7.2
*A sample of
a book*

Sample banner

Buy title from within the sample.

- Using your iCloud account, you can re-download any books you've purchased from the iBooks Store, regardless of which device you used to buy them. Switch to the Purchased Books collection and tap any title with an iCloud download button (🔲). That way you don't have to keep everything on one device, and more importantly, you can easily grab purchased books on all of your iOS devices.

tip Tap the More button at the top of the iBooks Store screen to locate books in various genres. You can also browse the *New York Times* bestseller list by tapping the NYTimes button in the toolbar.

note Books purchased from the iBooks Store are protected by Apple's FairPlay digital rights management (DRM) scheme, which means you can't give the book to someone else when you're finished reading it, as you can with a print book.

Import Your Own Ebooks

Books from the iBooks Store are formatted as EPUB files, an open format designed for electronic publishing by the International Digital Publishing Forum. Titles from Project Gutenberg (www.gutenberg.org) are all EPUB files, without Apple's DRM, and are available from other sources.

If you purchase or download an EPUB file, you can add the book to your iBooks library. In iTunes, choose File > Add to Library and locate the file. The book is added to the iPad the next time you sync. Or you can add a book without involving iTunes or syncing by downloading a file directly in Safari, emailing the file to yourself, and choosing Open In when selecting it in the Mail app. You could also use something like Dropbox or GoodReader to access the file from a shared folder, then choose Open In to specify the iBooks app.

note Before you purchase EPUB books online, make sure you know what you're buying. Not every EPUB file will work with iBooks. Titles from Kobo (www.kobobooks.com), for example, are EPUB formatted but are protected by Adobe DRM. (You can download the free Kobo app to read them.)

Creating Your Own EPUB Books

Writing a novel? Or perhaps you have an electronic book formatted as a text-only file? With the assistance of a few utilities, you can build your own EPUB files for viewing in iBooks (or any other reader that accepts the format). Here are a few examples:

- Pages, from Apple's iWork (www.apple.com/iwork/), allows you to export any document into the EPUB format for reading in iBooks.

- iBooks Author (www.apple.com/ibooks-author/) is Apple's free OS X app for developing media-rich textbooks and similar types of titles.

- Calibre (www.calibre-ebook.com) is an application available for Windows, OS X, and Linux that accepts several text formats and converts a document to an EPUB.

- Scrivener (www.literatureandlatte.com) for OS X and Windows is an excellent long-form writing tool with support for outputting EPUB files.

- Adobe InDesign (www.adobe.com) is the big gorilla in this zoo, with support for creating EPUB files.

Browse Your Library

Your books appear as front-facing covers in the iBooks library (**Figure 7.3**). Swipe up to reveal more books as your library grows.

Toggle Icon or List view.

Figure 7.3
The iBooks bookshelf

Should any of your collections get too full of titles, or you want a sorted view, tap the List view button (**Figure 7.4**). List view presents more options for organizing the library. Tap one of the buttons at the bottom of the screen to reorder the list.

Figure 7.4
Sort options in List view

 Titles in the Bookshelf List view can be reordered, deleted, and moved to different collections, just as they can in the main Bookshelf view.

Manage collections

Imagine a real-world library where all the books are stacked haphazardly in the middle of the floor. That's what the iBooks library could become, if not for collections and controls for organizing the titles. Right away, iBooks includes three collections: Books, for EPUB files; Purchased Books, for anything bought from the iBooks Store; and PDFs, for files in Portable Document Format. If you've added any PDF files to iBooks, view them by doing one of the following:

- Tap the Collections button, then tap the PDFs button to see them arranged on another shelf (**Figure 7.5**).

- Swipe right or left to switch between collection shelves.

Figure 7.5
Getting to the PDF shelf

> **note** To add PDFs to your iTunes library, simply drag and drop from your desktop into the iTunes application. You can also send PDFs to iBooks from the Mail app on the iPad: Touch and hold the PDF file in an email and choose Open In iBooks from the selection of compatible apps.

Rearrange or remove titles

Normally, books and PDFs appear in the order you add them to the library, with the most recent title appearing at the top-left location. You can move them around easily: Touch and hold a title, and drag it to a new spot.

To delete titles, do the following:

1. Tap the Edit button.

2. Select one or more titles by tapping their covers.

3. Tap the red Delete button (you'll be asked to confirm this deletion).

4. Tap Done to finish.

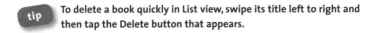

tip To delete a book quickly in List view, swipe its title left to right and then tap the Delete button that appears.

tip Books are backed up to your computer when you sync to iTunes. If you want to keep a book but remove it from the iPad's library, make sure you sync before deleting it from iBooks. If you back up the iPad to iCloud instead of iTunes, books are saved; however, restoring an iCloud backup requires restoring the entire device, so you can't just pluck a PDF from your backup.

Organize titles into collections

Collections let you do more than just separate books and PDFs—you can create multiple shelves based on whatever organizing criteria you come up with. For instance, you could separate biographies, science fiction, and historical romances on their own sets of shelves. To create a new collection, do the following:

1. Tap the Collections button, and then tap the New Collection button.

2. Type a name in the blank field that appears and tap Done (**Figure 7.6**).

Tapping the Edit button in the popover enables you to reorder or delete collections (although Books, Purchased Books, and PDFs can't be altered).

To view a collection, tap the Collections button and then tap that collection's name. Or, swipe left or right to switch among them.

Figure 7.6
Creating a new collection

Move titles to collections

After you've set up some collections, moving titles between them is similar to the steps for deleting books.

1. Tap the Edit button.

2. Tap to select the titles you wish to move.

3. Tap the Move button (**Figure 7.7**).

4. Tap the collection name to set the destination for the move. (You can also create a new collection at this step if you thought of a new categorization.) iBooks moves the titles and whisks you to that collection.

Figure 7.7
*Moving selected
titles to other
collections*

> **tip** Collections are agnostic as far as file format, allowing you to place books and PDFs side by side on a shelf.

> **tip** If you delete a title from a collection and then later decide to sync it back to your iPad, it will return to that collection. Also, if you delete a collection, you'll be asked whether you want to remove titles on that shelf from the iPad or move them to their original collection.

> **note** Keep the same collections across multiple iOS devices by turning on Sync Collections in Settings > iBooks.

Search for books

When the number of books in your library starts to get really out of control (or, as my stepsister would say, "A good start"), you can use the Search Books field hidden at the top of both the Bookshelf and List views to locate a title. Swipe down until you reach the top to reveal the search field in either view, tap inside the field, and then start typing a title or author name to narrow the list (**Figure 7.8**).

Figure 7.8
Searching your library

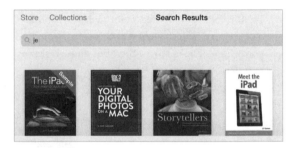

Read Books and PDFs

To open a book, tap its cover. The appearance of the book changes based on the iPad's rotation. When viewed in portrait orientation, you see one page at a time. Turn it to landscape orientation and the text is split over two pages.

> **tip** To keep the screen from rotating if you shift or change position, use your chosen method of locking the rotation—either using the side switch above the volume buttons or via Control Center. (See Chapter 1 to learn how to configure the side switch.)

Navigate a book

It feels a little funny that I should tell you how to read a book (obviously, you're doing a fine job reading my book), but there are a few things to note before you get absorbed by the content you're about to read.

- Tap the middle of the screen to reveal the reading controls if they're not visible. (Tap again to make them disappear.)

- To turn to the next page, swipe right to left. Swipe left to right to go to the previous page. You don't need to swipe the width of the page; a small swipe works the same.

  For kicks, drag the page edge slowly (**Figure 7.9**): Apple made a point of reproducing the look of curling the page, complete with a preview of what's on the next page (in landscape mode) or ghosted, reversed letters that would show through typical book-quality paper.

- Tap the right or left edge of the screen to turn the page using a faster, minimal animation.

Figure 7.9
Turning pages

Tap for previous page.   Tap for next page.

tip In the iBooks preferences (go to Settings > iBooks) is the option to specify what happens when you tap the left margin. By default it takes you to the previous page, but if you don't anticipate going backwards (you forward-thinking reader, you), tap the Both Margins Advance button. You can still go to the previous page by swiping left-to-right anywhere on the screen.

- Tap the Contents button (≡) to view the table of contents. You can tap a chapter or section to navigate to it, or tap the Resume button to go back to where you were.

- Drag the navigation control at the bottom of the screen to jump to a specific page or chapter (**Figure 7.10**).

Figure 7.10
Advancing to another section of the book

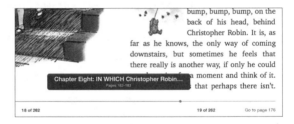

note As you're reading, the lower-right corner tells you how many pages are left in the current chapter. How many times have you been reading in bed, almost at the verge of sleep, but decided to push on until the end of the chapter? In iBooks, you don't have to flip ahead to see how much further ahead the next chapter is.

Navigate an illustrated book

iBooks can render fully illustrated books—such as children's picture books or fine art books—reproducing the "spread" layout of the original paper version, where illustrations can span across two opened pages.

While most of the navigation tools are similar to those for text-based titles, illustrated books get a few navigation enhancements.

- The navigation control at the bottom of the screen displays page previews rather than just page numbers. Tap it to reveal a larger popover preview, and drag to jump to a new page (**Figure 7.11**).

- Tap the Contents button to also view page previews.

- Double-tap to get a closer look at a page.

- Pinch with two fingers to zoom in and out.

Figure 7.11
Navigating an illustrated book

Navigate a PDF

Reading a PDF in iBooks is a bit like reading an illustrated book (minus the page-curling effect when you turn a page), but with a few differences.

- The navigation control at the bottom of the screen displays small thumbnails of the pages, but you don't get a larger preview popover.

- The reading controls at the top of the page are similar to those for EPUB books, save for the addition of a Share button, enabling you to attach the PDF to an email or send it to a printer.

note Unlike with books, you won't get a two-page spread when viewing a PDF in landscape view in iBooks. You'll have more control over page display if you use another PDF-compatible app, such as GoodReader.

Reading Books Aloud with VoiceOver

The iPad includes VoiceOver, an accessibility feature for people with limited vision that reads aloud text and the names of onscreen elements. It's also a way to have iBooks read a book while I'm cooking or doing some other hands-free activity.

To use VoiceOver, you'll have to do a little system-wide preference setup and learn a few new gestures to control the iPad. (I've also found it doesn't work in all books.) To give it a try, do the following:

1. Go to Settings > General > Accessiblity > Accessibility Shortcut and tap the VoiceOver option.

2. In a book within iBooks, triple-click the home button to turn VoiceOver on.

3. Tap once anywhere in the text and then drag down with two fingers to begin reading the page. When the end of the page is reached, it turns automatically and continues reading the next.

4. To pause at any time, tap the screen once with two fingers. Tapping again with two fingers restarts the reading.

Search Text

Another way to navigate a book or PDF is to look for occurrences of specific text (or, I suppose, another way to find out how many times an author swears throughout the text). The number of matches appears at the bottom of the results list. This feature also provides convenient Search Google and Search Wikipedia buttons to expand your search in Safari.

1. Tap the middle of the screen to display the reading controls.

2. Tap the Search button (Q) in the upper-right corner.

3. Type a search term, and tap the Search button on the onscreen keyboard or wait a few seconds for results to appear (**Figure 7.12**).

4. Scroll through the results to find the one you want, and then tap it to go to that place in the book. The term is highlighted so you can find it easily.

Figure 7.12
Searching the book

tip   When you tap the Search button again, the previous results are still available.

A slightly faster method of searching is available when you select a word or phrase on a page.

1. Touch and hold to select the text you want to find.

2. From the options that appear, tap the Search button (**Figure 7.13**). The search results popover appears.

Figure 7.13
Searching by selection

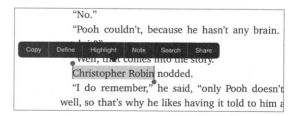

Change Appearance

Reading is a personal experience, and iBooks offers a few options for customizing the appearance of your books and PDFs.

Adjust screen brightness

The iPad's bright screen becomes a liability when it's flooding the bedroom with light and preventing your partner from sleeping or when it's intimidating the pets. Tap the Appearance button (ₐA) to expose a slider that changes the brightness level (**Figure 7.14**).

Figure 7.14
The Brightness slider

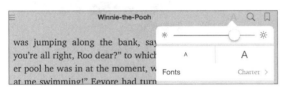

> **note** The Brightness setting in iBooks is applied system-wide, so it sticks when you leave the iBooks app. To bring the backlight level back up, swipe up from the bottom of the screen to open Control Center and adjust the brightness slider (or, open Settings > Wallpapers & Brightness).

Change theme

Another way to turn down the bright backlighting of the white page background is to change the theme. Tap the Appearance button (ₐA) and enable the Night (reversed) option. Or, if the white background is too stark, choose the Sepia option.

Enable Scrolling View

In the same popover, tap the Scrolling View button to remove the book's artificial page breaks and scroll the contents as you would a Web page.

Change text size and font

One noticeable advantage of electronic books is that you can adjust the type size to match what's comfortable for your eyes.

1. Tap the Appearance button ($_A$A) to display a popover with text options (**Figure 7.15**).

Figure 7.15
Adjusting text size and font

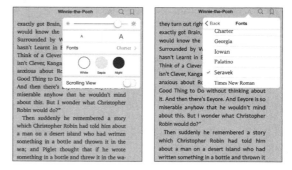

2. Tap the small A button to make the text smaller, or tap the large A button to make it larger.

3. Tap the Fonts button to reveal the typeface options.

4. Tap one of the font names to use that for the book's text.

5. Tap outside the popover to dismiss it.

tip If you feel more comfortable reading larger fonts, go to the iBooks preferences and turn off Full Justification to render paragraphs with a ragged right edge—which should improve readability at increased point sizes. If you keep Full Justification turned on, it's best to also keep Auto-hyphenation on to avoid some lines having too much space.

Use Bookmarks, Highlights, and Notes

iBooks offers a full toolset for jogging your memory after you've put the ebook down, including bookmarks, text highlighting, and the ability to add notes in the virtual page margins.

note For highlighting and note-taking capabilities in PDFs, you'll need to turn to an alternative app, such as GoodReader. See "Other Ebook Readers," later in this chapter.

Create a new bookmark

On a page with text you want to remember later, tap the Bookmark button (⬚), which turns red.

To remove a bookmark, simply tap the button again and the red color goes away.

Create a new highlight

Because text gets reflowed when you switch between portrait and landscape views, your bookmark placement might not end up where you thought it would. A more precise way to recall text or illustrations is to use the highlighting feature.

1. Touch and hold to select the text or illustration you want to highlight. By default, a single word or image is selected. Drag the selection handles to expand what you'll highlight.

2. From the options that appear, tap the Highlight button. The selected text is then colored like it was drawn over with a real highlighter pen.

3. The options change to reveal the options available (**Figure 7.16**). Tap the left-most button to choose a color or underline the selection.

Figure 7.16
Highlighting text

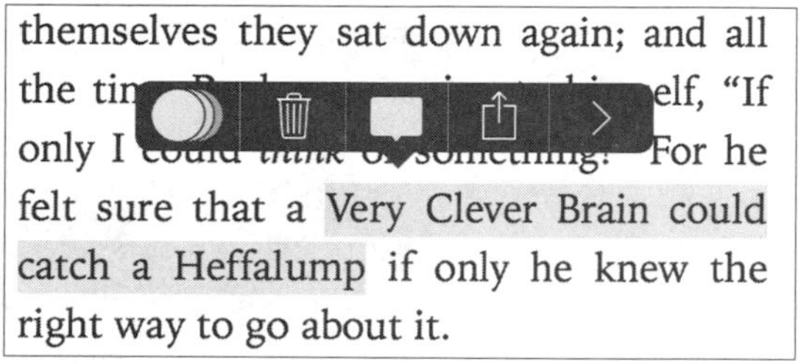

> themselves they sat down again; and all
> the time Pooh was saying to himself, "If
> only I could *think of something!* For he
> felt sure that a Very Clever Brain could
> catch a Heffalump if only he knew the
> right way to go about it.

Change highlight coloring

1. Tap on text or an image that's been highlighted.

2. From the options that appear, tap the color to use.

tip I like to categorize things by color, so the fact that you can change highlight colors makes me happy (as does the highlighter pen rendering). I'm sure the point is to simply let you choose your favorite color, but I can imagine two people sharing an iPad using colored bookmarks to read the same book. Or marking up text for different categories in a textbook, for example.

tip Tapping on highlighted material also brings up the option to remove the higlight (the Trash button)—something that was impossible to do in my old textbooks.

Create a new note

If something sparks an idea for next month's book club gathering, you can mark up your electronic book with notes. The process is similar to highlighting, except you get to add a virtual Post-it note to the page.

1. Touch and hold to select text or an illustration.

2. Tap the Note button from the options that appear. A square notepad appears, allowing you to type as long or as succinctly as you wish.

3. Tap outside the note when finished. A small colored note is added to the margin (**Figure 7.17**).

Figure 7.17
*A note in
the margin*

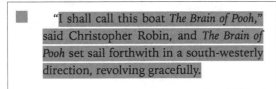

"I shall call this boat *The Brain of Pooh*," said Christopher Robin, and *The Brain of Pooh* set sail forthwith in a south-westerly direction, revolving gracefully.

Return to a bookmark, highlight, or note

When it's time to return to a placemarker or review your highlighting and notes, do the following:

1. Tap the Contents button to view the table of contents.

2. Tap the Bookmarks or Notes button.

3. Tap a bookmark, highlight, or note to go to that page (**Figure 7.18**).

Figure 7.18
Notes list

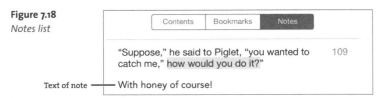

| Contents | Bookmarks | Notes |

"Suppose," he said to Piglet, "you wanted to catch me," how would you do it?"   109

Text of note ——— With honey of course!

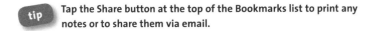

tip Tap the Share button at the top of the Bookmarks list to print any notes or to share them via email.

note Make sure your bookmarks, highlights, and notes are synchronized across all of your iOS devices by turning on Sync Bookmarks in Settings > iBooks.

Share a passage

If you come across a particularly interesting or moving section of a book and want the world to know, share it. Select a range of text, choose Share from the options that appear, and select a service (Message, Mail, Twitter, or Facebook). Or, choose Copy and paste the text into another app. You can also share notes from the Notes list:

1. With the Notes list visible, tap the Share button (🗍) .

2. Tap the Edit Notes button.

3. Tap to select one or more notes and highlights.

4. Tap the Share button (the text version) and choose Mail to create a new outgoing message that includes the note and a link to the book if it's available in the iBooks Store.

Look Up Word Definitions

One of the great joys (and sometimes great frustrations) of reading is coming across unfamiliar words. iBooks offers a built-in dictionary.

1. Touch and hold a word to select it.

2. From the options that appear, tap the Define button. (The first time you do this, you'll need to download a dictionary from a provided list.) A definition appears (**Figure 7.19**).

Figure 7.19
*Viewing a
definition*

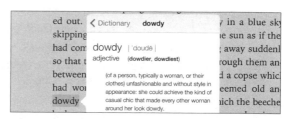

Other Ebook Readers

iBooks is the Apple-designed option, but of course a plethora of other ebook reading applications are out there (such as a little Amazon.com offering you may have heard of). Publishers are also writing iPad *apps*, not just book files, that do so much more than turn pages.

- **Kindle for iPad.** When people think of Amazon's Kindle, they picture the hardware: slim devices with grayscale E Ink screens that store lots of ebooks and have great battery life. What they may forget is that Amazon offers Kindle for iPad, a free app that brings the reading experience to the iPad. It's a great alternative if you're already using Amazon for purchases.

- **Barnes & Noble Nook.** Barnes & Noble got into the e-reader market with its Nook devices and multi-platform software, including two apps for the iPad. The Nook for iPad app differentiates itself with more choices for text rendering and layout. You can customize both text and page colors and save those combinations as themes, as well as modify leading (the space between lines) and margins. Barnes & Noble was also the first company to allow you to lend titles to others who have Nook devices or software, though not every title is available to lend (it's up to the publisher to decide); Amazon has followed suit with a similar two-week lending feature.

- **Ebooks from public libraries.** Voracious library users might feel a shock to the pocketbook, as the switch from free borrowing to ebook ownership can put a dent in the entertainment budget. But there's hope for the book hungry, as more libraries are now lending ebooks.

  Bluefire Reader (www.bluefirereader.com/bluefire-reader.html) reads files protected by Adobe DRM. OverDrive Media Console (www.overdrive.com) ties into a network of libraries.

- **Standalone apps.** Publishers also offer standalone apps for books that include not only the core text, but other multimedia content. For example, many children's books have options to read the story aloud, play games, and color on the screen. Reference works, such as *The Elements: A Visual Exploration*, can convey much more information than the facts and some photos.

- **Comic books.** Since its release, I can't tell you how many reviewers (myself included) have pointed out that the iPad could be the enticement that makes them start reading comics again. Apps like ComiXology, Marvel, DC, Comics Plus, and IDW Comics provide the framework for reading and then let you purchase issues in the app. Apple has now started offering comics and graphic novels in the iBooks Store, too.

- **Read PDF files and more with GoodReader.** Download the reader to rule them all. GoodReader (www.goodiware.com) is one of those apps that do so much you feel like you're just scratching the surface. A more powerful PDF viewer than iBooks, GoodReader offers more options for viewing PDFs (including orientation adjustment and double pages) and can mark up pages (from highlighting and notes to drawing figures and underlining text).

  In addition to viewing these static files, you can also play a wide range of video and audio files as well as view Web archives (which bundle all text and images from Web pages and preserve their original layout) saved from Safari on your Mac or Windows PC.

  You can import files by using the drag-and-drop interface in the Apps pane within iTunes, by transferring files over a Wi-Fi network, by downloading from the Web, and even by accessing your Dropbox account. It preserves Web links, lets you add bookmarks, allows you to password-protect files, and so much more than I have room to go into here.

Read Magazines with Newsstand

Do your reading tastes veer more toward magazines? Newsstand provides an interface for getting and reading iPad versions of popular magazines as well as original magazines created just for electronic distribution. Tap the Newsstand icon to reveal magazines (**Figure 7.20**), and tap the Store button to locate others.

Figure 7.20
Newsstand

The magazines themselves are actually standalone apps that register as Newsstand items. The difference is that many magazines and newspapers can automatically download updates or alert you with notifications when new content is available. Also note that most magazines are free to download, but to actually read any content you must subscribe or buy issues within the apps.

Entertain Yourself

Laptops took computing off the desk and made it more portable, but using one for enjoyable pursuits like watching movies always feels a bit like work. It's as if you went to the theater and got seated in a cubicle. The keyboard is in the way, and with most laptops you find yourself scrambling to find and plug in the power cord right as something exciting is happening in the movie.

On the iPad, the movie takes over the entire device, without computer clutter getting in the way. Your music library is a few taps away. YouTube movies are ready to be streamed. AirPlay lets you watch movies on an Apple TV instantly. And Home Sharing makes it possible to play media from any computer on your network, no syncing required. As I discuss elsewhere in the book, the iPad can be incredibly productive, but it can also be a lot of fun.

Sync Media

It is odd that we use i*Tunes* as the central hub for syncing all information to the iPad, but during the early years of the iPod the only data to sync were music files. Since then, our music and movie libraries have grown alongside the capacities of Apple's players, using iTunes as the store-house for most of our digital entertainment. I've already covered the basics of syncing in Chapter 1, so in this section I'll highlight sync options that pertain specifically to music, videos, audiobooks, and podcasts.

note It's finally possible to manage your media without using iTunes as a middleman, thanks to iTunes Match and iCloud. If you've taken that route, see "Sync Media Using iTunes Match" a few pages ahead.

Choose which media to sync

Depending upon the size of your iTunes media library, you may have no trouble synchronizing everything to the iPad (which is the default setting). But even if there is room, you may want to be more choosy about how you fill those bytes (so you're not stumbling over your collection of kids' music while on a business trip, for example).

1. Connect the iPad to your computer and, in iTunes, select it from the Devices list.

2. Click the Music tab.

3. Ensure that the Sync Music checkbox is enabled, and choose the radio button for "Selected playlists, artists, albums, and genres" (**Figure 8.1**).

4. Choose any of the following options (or ignore them and go to the next step):

   ▪ **Include music videos:** You can purchase music videos from the iTunes Store, and some albums include videos as bonus material.

With this box checked, the videos are copied along with the music. If a video comes up when listening to an album, just the music plays.

- **Include voice memos:** This option is a holdover from the iPhone, which includes a Voice Memos application.

- **Automatically fill free space with songs:** You bought a 128 GB iPad and don't want to waste any free space? This option packs the memory full of music beyond what you specify in the fields below.

Figure 8.1

Syncing music in iTunes

5. In the Playlists, Artists, Genres, and Albums lists, click checkboxes belonging to any items you wish to transfer to the iPad. Use the search field at the top of the Music pane to find matches quickly.

6. Click the Apply button to sync with the new options.

> **tip** To quickly select or deselect all items in one of the lists, Command-click (or Control-click under Windows) a checkbox.

tip Two general sync settings that appear on the iPad summary pane in iTunes let you fit more media onto the device. "Convert higher bit rate songs to [128/192/256] kbps AAC" downsamples audio to one of three lower qualities (you choose which), reducing the songs' files sizes. "Prefer standard definition videos" leaves larger-sized HD movies on your computer and transfers only standard-definition ones.

note The "Manually manage music and videos" option lets you drag songs and video from your library to the iPad in the sidebar, which is fine if your media library isn't too large. But these days, I'd rather specify playlists than micromanage every file.

Create a Smart Playlist in iTunes

A normal playlist contains a fixed set of songs that you add manually. A *Smart* Playlist generates its content based on criteria you specify. For example, you could sync a Smart Playlist that includes any media that's been added to iTunes within the last month. Here's how to build it:

1. In iTunes, choose File > New > Smart Playlist.

2. From the pop-up menu, choose a selector and conditions (**Figure 8.2**).

Figure 8.2
*Creating a
Smart Playlist
in Tunes*

3. Click the + button to add more selectors, which determine what results appear. You can also nest conditions by Option-clicking (Mac) or Alt-clicking (Windows) the + button. Nesting allows you to specify that any or all of a given set of attributes is matched. For example,

in addition to locating songs added in the last month, you could also specify that the genre is not Classical or Soundtrack and that the media kind is not Audiobook.

4. Click OK to save the Smart Playlist.

5. Give the playlist a name.

The next time you set up your sync criteria when the iPad is connected, include that playlist. Each time you sync, the playlist is updated with new songs.

Sync Media Using iTunes Match

Apple's iTunes Match is an interesting service: For $24.99 a year, you can download any song you own, whether you bought it from the iTunes Store, bought it from another retailer, or ripped it from a CD. What's the point if you already have that music? Let's say you bought a 16 GB iPad, and the free space is quickly disappearing as you add movies, photos, and other large files. You don't need to store your entire iTunes library on the iPad—just stream or download the songs you feel like listening to.

After you sign up for the service in iTunes, the application compares your library with the database of songs offered by Apple (the "match" in iTunes Match). Anything not matched is uploaded, so even if you delete a bootleg concert recording, you can re-download it later. (The matching process can take quite a while, so I suggest you let it run overnight or longer; you'll still be able to use iTunes and play your music.)

Once you're set up with the service, go to Settings > Music on your iPad and turn on the iTunes Match option. Any music already stored on the device is erased and replaced by a listing of your full library.

Unfortunately, iTunes Match is currently limited to 25,000 songs. If your library is larger than that, you need to trim it.

Download iTunes Match tracks

iTunes Match tracks can be streamed, but that doesn't help if you're in an area with no Internet access (or you don't want to eat up the bandwidth on your cellular plan if you own a cellular-capable iPad). In that case, download it from iTunes using any of the following options:

- Tap the iCloud download button (**Figure 8.3**), which appears in all views except the Songs list. Tracks are transferred to your iPad but don't play. (Tap the download progress indicator if you want to cancel the transfer.)

- Tap a song to begin downloading and playing it. When that song ends, the next one in the list (whether you're viewing an album, a playlist, or the full song list) automatically plays next.

 The Music app can display just the items you've downloaded. Go to Settings > Music and turn the Show All Music option off.

Downloading   iCloud download

Figure 8.3
An album with iTunes Match enabled

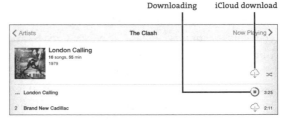

 Downloading your music consumes bandwidth, obviously, which you may not want to sacrifice if you own an iPad with cellular Internet service. If that's the case, go to Settings > iTunes & App Store, and turn off the Use Cellular Data option.

Upgrade low-quality songs

Having your entire music library available on any iOS device is great, but iTunes Match also has another feature that's worth its subscription price. Any track you download is formatted as a 256 kbps AAC file and isn't encumbered by digital rights management. That means you can download higher-quality files than what you may already have, at no extra cost. I wrote an article in *TidBITS* that covers the full details, including setting up Smart Playlists to find songs: http://tidbits.com/article/12872.

tip When your iPad fills up, the Music app deletes older, less-played songs automatically as needed. If you need to clear out space manually, the only alternative is to nuke your music library from orbit: Go to Settings > General > Usage > Music. Swipe across the All Music item and tap the Delete button that appears. All local music files are erased.

Play Music

If you're familiar with iTunes, you'll have no trouble playing music in the Music app. That said, the Music interface has a few peculiarities.

1. Tap a button at the bottom of the screen to view your library by playlist, song, artist, album, genre, or (under More) composer or compilation.

2. Tap the name of a song to start playing it. The listing determines how you get to that point:

   ■ **Songs:** The song list is arranged alphabetically, so the songs will play back in that order.

   ■ **Artists:** Tap an artist's name to view songs, arranged according to the albums on which they appear.

- **Albums:** Tap an album cover to view its songs, then tap a song to start playing. Albums are listed alphabetically by album title (**Figure 8.4**).

Figure 8.4
A track list in Albums view

- **Genres:** Tap the icon for a genre to view albums and songs of that musical style. The songs are listed alphabetically by song title (and surprisingly, the order can't be changed unless you turn on Shuffle for playback).

- **Composers:** Tap the name of a composer to view songs he or she has composed, then tap a song to begin playing. When multiple albums appear, playback ends when the album does.

The Music app also has a Now Playing screen, which presents the song's album art, full screen (**Figure 8.5**). In addition to offering controls for music playback and volume, the Now Playing screen includes a button in the upper-right corner to view the tracks belonging to the song's album; you can also double-tap the screen to do this. To return to Library view (without stopping playback), tap the button in the upper-left corner.

tip The Now Playing screen is the only location where you can rate a song. Tap the screen to reveal the rating control In place of the song title. Then tap a rating (from one to five stars) for the currently playing track.

Figure 8.5
Now Playing screen

Return to Library view   View album tracks

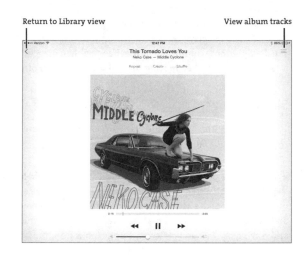

Navigate songs

While you're listening to audio, use the following controls to skip tracks, rewind, or fast-forward through a song (**Figure 8.6**).

Previous   Play/Pause   Next   Playhead

Figure 8.6
Playback controls

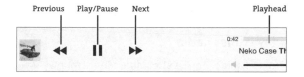

- Tap the Play/Pause button to start or stop playback.

- Tap the Previous button once to return to the beginning of the current song. Tap it twice to play the previous song in the list.

- Tap the Next button once to skip to the next song.

- Touch and hold the Previous or Next button to rewind or fast-forward through a track; holding the button longer speeds up playback.

- Drag the playhead to "scrub" to another section of a track.

tip For more control when scrubbing in the Now Playing screen, touch and hold the playhead and then drag your finger *down*. The farther down you drag, the more control you have when you then drag left or right. This feature is especially useful when moving through audiobooks or other lengthy tracks.

Shuffle songs

To introduce some randomness into your music listening, set your library to shuffle mode. While playing any song, tap the Shuffle button.

tip If you own an iPhone or iPod touch, you're probably familiar with the shake-to-shuffle feature: Simply shake the device, and the accelerometer recognizes the action and switches to shuffle play mode. The Music app on the iPad doesn't support that feature—believe me, I tried shaking, twisting, and waving my iPad and only got strange looks from the other people on the bus. My guess is that the iPad is just large enough that shaking isn't as practical when listening to music, so Apple didn't include the feature.

Repeat playback

Do you have a favorite album that begs to be repeated? In the Now Playing screen, tap the Repeat button and choose Repeat Song or Repeat Album.

Play iTunes Radio

iTunes Radio is Apple's streaming service for playing music that you don't own but would be interested in. (It's also a reaction to popular services such as Spotify and Pandora, both of which offer iOS apps.) Tap a Featured Station to explore music that Apple is recommending, or create your own station (**Figure 8.7**). Tap a station to start playback.

While songs are playing, you can purchase a track by tapping the price button in the upper-right corner of the screen.

To create a new station, tap the big New Station button and enter an artist, genre, or song in the text field that appears. You can also tap a genre from the list below to browse existing stations.

Or, while you're listening to a song, tap the Create button and choose New Station from Artist or New Station from Song.

Figure 8.7
iTunes Radio

 When you sign up for iTunes Match, you don't hear ads when playing iTunes Radio.

Play Genius Mixes

iTunes includes a feature called Genius Mixes, which assemble playlists based on the contents of your music library. Tap the Genius button and then tap a mix to start playing it. Unlike when playing other albums, you can't see (or edit) which songs are included in a Genius Mix—you just have to trust the algorithms (which often do a pretty good job).

Listen to audiobooks

Audiobooks use the same playback controls as other audio tracks, but they gain a few extra features. While listening to an audiobook, tap the Now Playing button to access the following controls:

■ **Change reading speed:** Since most podcasts and audiobooks are spoken-word performances, your ears are more sympathetic to other playback speeds. Tap the speed indicator below the track title to switch between 1x Speed (normal), 2x Speed (twice as fast), or 0.5x Speed (half of normal).

■ **Rewind or fast-forward in specific increments:** Did you miss what someone said? Tap the ⟲ button to move the playhead back 15 seconds, or the ⟳ button to advance 15 seconds.

> **tip** When I'm working on my computer, I almost always have music playing. And if I need to leave, I often want to continue listening to it. A clever utility called Seamless (http://fivedetails.com/seamless/) lets me transfer the audio from the computer to my iPad or iPhone without breaking a beat.

Create Music Playlists

You can build your own playlists in the Music app, which get synced back to iTunes the next time you connect.

Build a playlist

For a handpicked playlist, do the following:

1. Tap the Playlists button at the bottom of the screen.

2. Tap the New Playlist button.

3. Enter a name for the playlist in the dialog that appears, and tap Save.

4. Locate a song you want to add in the list, or tap the Artists, Albums, or Composers button to narrow your search.

5. Tap the Add All Songs button to include everything listed, or tap a song's ⊕ button to add that song to the playlist. The track title becomes gray to indicate it has been included (**Figure 8.8**).

Figure 8.8
Building a playlist

Track added ── to playlist

6. Tap Done to save the playlist.

 Tap the Edit button that appears at the top of a playlist's track listing if you want to add, delete, or rearrange songs.

Create a Genius playlist

That was quite a lot of work—what if the Music app could build a custom playlist for you? When you're listening to any song, tap the Create button and choose Genius Playlist. A set of songs based on the first one appears as a new Genius playlist (**Figure 8.9**).

Figure 8.9
A Genius playlist

Tap the Refresh button to generate a new list based on the original criteria. If you enjoyed the list, tap the Save button to turn it into a new, regular playlist.

Play Videos

I love movies, but I don't get out to see them often enough. And while there are a few flicks I'd prefer to see with a large group of people, I'm happy to catch up on my movie watching at home on my own time. The iPad is great for watching a movie (or TV show, or video podcast, or movie you created) when it's most convenient.

Video sync options

Syncing video works the same as syncing music, outlined earlier in the chapter, with one helpful difference. iTunes can automatically sync items that match timely criteria, such as the five most recent unwatched movies or the three most recently added items.

1. Connect the iPad and then, in iTunes, go to the Movies tab.

2. Click the checkbox for Automatically Include, and choose a range of items to copy to the iPad (**Figure 8.10**). (Of course, you can also choose not to include any movies automatically.)

Figure 8.10
Movies sync options

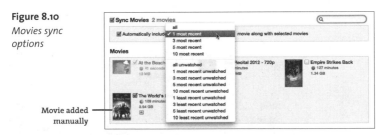

Movie added manually

3. In the Movies area that lists all available videos, click the checkbox for any item you want copied in addition to the automatic options. You can also choose movies that appear in iTunes playlists. Mark any items in the Include Movies from Playlists area.

4. Click the Apply button to sync the iPad and copy the movies.

Watch a movie

Your content is available in the Videos app on the iPad, with different categories split among panes (Rentals, Movies, TV Shows, Music Videos, and Home Videos, depending on what's in your library) (**Figure 8.11**).

Figure 8.11
Available movies

1. Tap a video's icon to view more information about it.

2. To begin playing the movie, tap the Play button (**Figure 8.12**). Depending on the content, you can optionally tap the Chapters button to jump ahead to specific sections.

Figure 8.12
Movie info

Play button

3. Sit back and enjoy the movie. If you need to interact with playback, tap the screen once to make the onscreen controls appear (**Figure 8.13**):

   - Use the playback controls to play, pause, rewind, or fast-forward. They operate similarly to the music controls explained earlier, though tapping once on the Rewind or Fast-forward buttons in long movies skips the video in 5-minute increments.

   - Drag the volume slider to increase or decrease the sound, or use the volume buttons on the iPad case.

   - Drag the playhead to scrub through the movie.

Fill Frame

Figure 8.13
Video controls

Volume slider   Playback controls   Subtitles

   - When watching widescreen movies, tap the Fill Frame button to use the entire screen (at the expense of cutting off the left and right edges of the picture).

   - Tap the Subtitles button to view captions (if available).

   - Tap Done to return to the movie info screen.

Buy or Rent a Video

To buy or rent movies and television shows, go to the iTunes Store in iTunes on your computer or tap the iTunes app on your iPad. Searching for and purchasing videos is similar to buying other things from the iTunes storefronts, but with a few annoying restrictions.

- The iPad and iPad mini can play HD movies, but some titles can only be purchased in SD (standard definition), some can be rented or purchased in SD, and some can be rented in HD only on the iPad. This crazy and confusing distinction is the result of the movies' rights holders (Hollywood studios) trying to wring profit, establish some measure of misguided control, or...well, to be honest I don't know. What's worse is that the availability of these options changes over time; some movies previously available for rent can only be purchased, or no longer appear in the iTunes Store. What this means for you and me is that we need to make sure we examine what we're about to purchase or rent.

- HD movies you rented on the iPad can be viewed only on the iPad, not transferred to your computer or another device. HD movies you rent in iTunes on your computer can be transferred to the iPad—but sometimes the HD version is available only on the iPad. (However, AirPlay helps in this regard, as I'll discuss shortly.)

- After renting a movie, you must watch it within 30 days. If you don't, the movie is automatically deleted from your library.

- Once you begin to watch a rental, you must finish watching it within 24 hours, after which point it's deleted.

note I apologize for sounding cranky, but I should be able to purchase a movie—in SD or HD, if available—and watch it wherever I want, especially if it's within Apple's ecosystem. As it is, Apple and the studios are making it difficult for people like me to give them money that I'm willing to part with in exchange for entertainment, which is a terrible business model.

Download or stream previously purchased videos

Apple uses your Apple ID to remember everything you've purchased from the iTunes Store. It's a bit of accounting that doesn't come as a surprise, except for one thing: You can re-download almost anything you've purchased.

1. On the iPad, open the Videos app. Movies available for iCloud streaming display an iCloud icon in the lower-right corner (see Figure 8.11 on page 187).

2. Tap the movie to view its information.

3. To stream the movie, tap the Play button. If you want to download and store it on the iPad, tap the iCloud download button.

tip This feature gets better: If you earlier bought an HD movie, the copy you have is probably at 720p resolution. If the movie is now available at 1080p, you can download the higher-quality version for free.

note You can also download purchased movies in the iTunes Store app. Tap the Purchased button to see which ones are available.

Watch Your Own Movies

The iTunes Store isn't the only source of movies, of course. Home movies you shoot and edit can be viewed on the iPad, too. Export them from your video editing software (such as iMovie or Windows Live Movie Maker) to iTunes as .m4v, .mp4, or .mov files. Once in iTunes, movies can be synced to the iPad.

tip You don't even need a desktop computer to edit your home movies. The iMovie app for iOS, free with a new iPad or just $4.99 if you own an older iPad, is a versatile editor on your iPad or iPad mini (or iPhone).

Convert DVDs

What about movies you already own on DVD? Using software such as HandBrake (www.handbrake.fr), you can convert a movie to a digital file that can be imported into iTunes and synced to the iPad. This option is great if you're going on a long trip and don't want to bring along a stack of DVDs, or for storing kids' entertainment when you don't want the original disc to be damaged. (The iPad is already a favorite for kids and parents—I know from experience—on lengthy car or plane trips.)

note It's worth pointing out here that I'm not a lawyer, and that the practice of encoding DVDs is technically against the law in the United States due to the Digital Millennium Copyright Act (DMCA). Making digital copies of movies you've legally purchased seems like a legitimate fair use to me, and is far preferable to downloading questionably ripped movies from the Internet. The Electronic Frontier Foundation provides more information about the topic (www.eff.org/issues/drm).

Stream Media Between Devices

The iPad's screen is great for watching movies—I've invested plenty of testing hours to verify the claim—but movies were meant to be viewed on even larger screens. Streaming also applies to watching video or listening to music that's stored on another computer nearby.

AirPlay

If you have a second- or third-generation Apple TV (the small, black unit), you can play a video directly between the iPad and the Apple TV by tapping one button. AirPlay also works for playing music to the Apple TV or to an AirPort Express connected to a stereo.

If an Apple TV or AirPort Express is on the same Wi-Fi network as your iPad, an AirPlay button appears near the playback controls.

1. Begin playing a video or song. This feature isn't limited to just the Videos and Music apps; most apps that can display media, such as Safari, can play media on other devices using AirPlay.

2. Tap the AirPlay button (**Figure 8.14**).

Figure 8.14
Choosing an AirPlay source in the Videos app

AirPlay button

3. Choose an AirPlay device from the list that appears. After a few seconds, for video, the picture disappears from the iPad and starts playing on the television, right where you left off.

4. When you want to resume playing the media on your iPad, tap the button and choose iPad from the popover.

Home Sharing

Over the years, I've accumulated movies, TV shows, and music that now reside on a large hard drive attached to a computer at home. In the past, syncing files to watch was a hassle, but now I can access it all through Apple's Home Sharing feature. Specify your Apple ID on the iPad to stream content from computers on your network.

tip You need to set the same Apple ID for all devices on your network that will use Home Sharing.

Set up Home Sharing

Do the following to enable Home Sharing on the iPad:

1. Open Settings > Music or Settings > Videos (either option works).

2. Under Home Sharing, enter your Apple ID and password.

3. Tap Done on the onscreen keyboard.

Play media stored on another machine

To play media via Home Sharing, do the following:

1. Open the Music or Videos app (depending on what you want to play).

2. In Music, tap the More button and then the Shared button
   (**Figure 8.15**); in Videos, tap the Shared button at the top of the screen.

Figure 8.15
Access a shared library using Home Sharing

3. Tap the name of the shared library you want to access.

4. Locate the media you want to play, just as if the content were stored on your iPad.

5. If you want to disconnect from the computer, tap the name of the active library in Music or return to the main screen in Videos.

> **tip** Another option for home streaming is to run an app such as AirVideo or StreamToMe. These apps don't require an Apple ID, and you can specify media sources (such as additional folders) outside iTunes.

Streaming-video services

Members of the movie rental service Netflix can download the free Netflix app for the iPad and take advantage of the company's growing library of Watch Now titles. Amazon.com also offers its Amazon Instant Video app for members of its Prime service.

Other popular options are the ABC Player app and the PBS for iPad app, which provide streaming versions of the networks' programs. Episodes are typically available the day after they air on broadcast television. As another example, Hulu Plus members can download a free app to watch other TV programs.

Play Videos on a Television Using Cables

AirPlay over a wireless network isn't the only option for playing videos on the TV. There are six options, depending on the TV's connectors. For iPads and iPad minis with the Lightning connector, a Lightning to Digital AV Adapter (HDMI) and Lightning to VGA Adapter are available. Other iPads can use the Digital AV Adapter (HDMI), the Component AV Cable Kit, the Composite AV Cable Kit, and the iPad Dock Connector to VGA Adapter. The HDMI adapters and the component kit have the advantage of being digital, versus analog, so they enable you to play protected content (such as videos bought from the iTunes Store).

Although the iPad can play back 1080p HD video, some of the kits don't offer it. The component kit offers 576p (usually 720 by 576 pixels) and 480p (usually 640 by 480); the composite kit handles 576i and 480i (the same resolutions, but interlaced instead of progressive-scan). The HDMI adapter can do 1080p from the iPad.

9

Find Yourself with Maps

If anything about the iPad makes me feel like I'm living in the future (well, there are a lot of things), it's the Maps app. Within a few seconds, I can look up an address, find a nearby business, go virtual sightseeing with my daughter, or get directions from my current location—wherever that happens to be—to any address. The iPad Wi-Fi + cellular models include a GPS chip for accurate location discovery, but the Wi-Fi–only models can also use Maps well.

Unlike older versions, which relied on Google's mapping information, Maps under iOS 7 is a new effort—home-brewed by Apple. Unfortunately, it ran into snags with the data when first released, so Maps quickly became a punchline. The good news is that the data is constantly being improved; I see fewer glitches, and I've used the turn-by-turn directions many times without incident.

Find Yourself

For a quick taste of what the Maps app can do, launch it and tap the Current Location button (⌀). The first time you do this, Maps asks for your permission to use your location.

The map zooms in, indicating your location with a blue circle (**Figure 9.1**). A pale circle emanating from the sphere represents how accurate the location is: A large circle means you're located somewhere within that area. If you see no circle (other than a faint pulse to make the sphere more visible), it means the iPad has pinpointed its location.

Figure 9.1
Finding a location in Maps

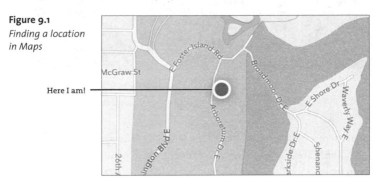

Here I am!

To navigate the map, do any of the following:

- Drag with one finger to reposition the map. As you move around, the map redraws areas previously outside the borders of the frame. At any time, you can tap the Current Location button to re-center the map on your position.

- Pinch two fingers to zoom in or out. You can pinch and move at the same time, too.

- Double-tap anywhere on the screen to zoom in on that area.

- All iPad models include a compass, a chip that can determine which direction it's pointed. Tap the Current Location button again to orient the view according to the direction you're facing (**Figure 9.2**).

Figure 9.2
Compass view

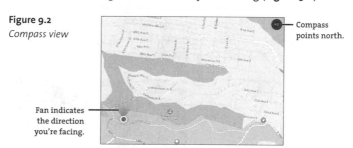

Compass points north.

Fan indicates the direction you're facing.

tip The compass works best when the iPad is held flat, parallel to the ground. You may need to recalibrate it occasionally using a software tool that will appear when needed.

Location Services: How the iPad Knows Position

The cellular iPad models include a chip that picks up GPS (Global Positioning Satellite) signals and translates them into an accurate physical location. The Wi-Fi–only models do not contain a GPS chip, but Maps still works. How?

Apple designed a system it calls Location Services, which takes GPS and cellular location data (if available) to come up with an accurate fix on your position. It's possible to reset Location Services (in case you accidentally tapped Don't Allow for an app), although it clears all permissions; you'll need to grant access to apps again the next time they ask. Go to Settings > General > Reset, and tap the Reset Location & Privacy button. You can also disable Location Services in Settings > Privacy or turn it off for specific apps.

Map views

The Maps app offers three map views that cater to people who find routes in different ways. If you feel turned around using the Standard style, you may find it helpful to see landmarks in Hybrid or Satellite view, for instance. To access the styles, tap the information button (ⓘ) at the lower-right corner of the screen. Tap a style to switch to it (**Figure 9.3**).

Figure 9.3
A composite of the map styles

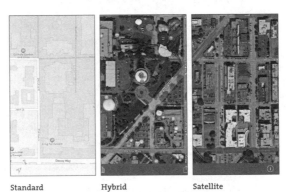

Standard   Hybrid   Satellite

The Maps app also features what Apple calls Flyover, a 3D view of the map that includes detailed photo-textured buildings and other objects. Tap the 3D button in Standard view; in Hybrid and Satellite views, the button looks like a trio of buildings (**Figure 9.4**).

Figure 9.4
Flyover mode

Flyover button ——————

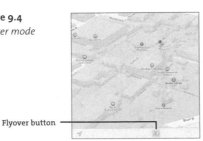

Navigating in Flyover mode is the same as in the regular mode (pinch to zoom, for instance), with a couple of additions:

- Drag vertically with two fingers to adjust the angle of view to appear closer to the ground or higher above.

- Rotate two fingers on the screen as if you were turning a knob to rotate around the view's center axis (**Figure 9.5**).

Figure 9.5
Flyover gestures

Change vertical angle   Rotate around axis

 Instead of first tapping the Flyover button, drag vertically with two fingers to switch from the top-down view to Flyover mode.

Find Locations

Now that you know where you are, it's time to go exploring. The search field can accept nearly any query, not just addresses. Type "coffee," for example, and results appear as red pins on the map. You can also start typing a specific company name, the name of a person or company in your Contacts list, or the name of an earlier search result.

Tap a pin to identify the location (**Figure 9.6**, on the next page). If you don't see what you're looking for, the match may be outside the current screen view. Tap the ☰ button to display a popover containing a list of the results.

Figure 9.6
*Search results
as pins*

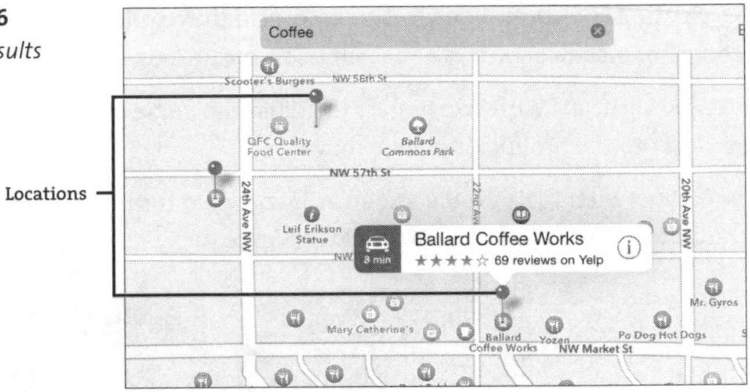

Locations —

Get information about a location

To learn more about a location, tap the ⓘ button. The label expands to
display more information and options (**Figure 9.7**).

Figure 9.7
*More information
about a location*

- Tap the Home Page label to visit the site in Safari.
- Tap the Create New Contact button to create a new contact record
  containing all of the information.

- Tap the Share button and choose whether to send the information via Mail, Messages, Twitter, or Facebook. The message contains a URL to view the location on Google Maps in a Web browser, the location as a vCard file (for easy import into most address book applications), or both, depending on the service. Another option is AirDrop, which opens the location in the Maps app on the iOS device that receives it.

- Tap Add Bookmark to save the location for the future. It will be available by tapping the Bookmarks button in the toolbar.

- Tap one of the Directions buttons to view a route to the location; see "Get Directions," coming up in this chapter.

- Touch and hold any field, and then tap the Copy option that appears to copy just that information for pasting elsewhere (such as in an outgoing email message).

- Tap the Report a Problem button if something about the location information needs to be corrected.

Drop a pin

In addition to finding locations through a search, you can drop a pin on an arbitrary location to get more information about it or to mark a spot for reference.

1. Touch and hold an area of the screen. A purple pin lands there, with the address of the location listed in its label (**Figure 9.8**).

Figure 9.8
Dropped pin

2. Touch and hold the pin to lift it from the map, and then drag it to a more specific location if you want. Tapping the ⓘ icon reveals the options for copying and saving the address.

To remove a pin, tap the ⓘ icon and then tap the Remove Pin button.

If you touch and hold the screen to drop a new pin, the previous one disappears. You can have only one purple pin on the map at one time.

Get Directions

I used to think that getting and printing directions from a mapping service on my computer was pretty cool, but now I don't even bother with the paper. It's easy to get directions between two locations in the Maps app—and not just driving directions, but walking routes, too. (Maps also displays a button for getting public transit directions, but tapping it leads only to a list of third-party transit apps in the App Store.)

1. Tap the Directions button in the upper-left corner to switch to Directions mode. A popover appears with two fields: the starting point and the destination. The iPad assumes you want to start at your current location, but you can replace that text and search for another.

   If you already performed a search, tap the car icon to the left of the search result label.

2. Enter a destination by doing a search in the second field (**Figure 9.9**).

Figure 9.9
Searching for a destination

To change the starting point, tap the first field and enter a search term or address. If you had previously dropped a pin, you can select its location by tapping the first field and selecting the address in purple text.

3. Tap Route on the onscreen keyboard to reveal the route, which appears as a blue line between the two points (**Figure 9.10**). For easier identification, the starting point is a green pin and the destination is a red pin.

4. If multiple routes are offered, tap one to choose it.

Figure 9.10
*Destination,
known*

Suggested route ——————

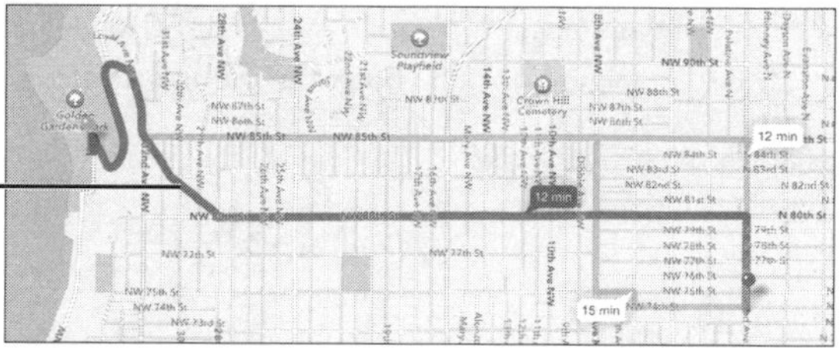

tip   The iPad Air and Retina iPad mini each contain a dedicated chip that records movement, the M7 motion co-processor. (Because it's a dedicated chip, it uses very little battery power.) It can detect when you've parked your car and will switch to walking directions to guide you the rest of the way to your destination.

tip   If you're viewing information about an address, tap the Directions From Here or Directions To Here button to initiate a search.

tip   I find myself often turning to Siri for directions. For example, after activating Siri I say, "Take me to the Space Needle." That jumps right to the directions interface.

Follow the directions

As you travel, the Maps app can give you step-by-step directions. If you own a cellular-enabled iPad or iPad mini and are leaving from your current location, Maps guides you using a real-time 3D map of the road and Siri's voice for speaking prompts and directions. Wi-Fi–only models offer steps superimposed over the route.

1. Tap the Start button in the directions bar.

2. On cellular iPads, simply follow Siri's directions—and pay attention to the road (**Figure 9.11**)! If you get off course, Maps plots a new route.

Figure 9.11
Guided by Siri

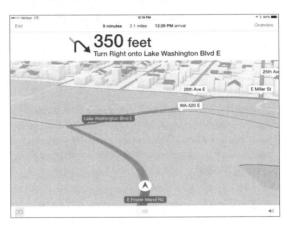

On Wi-Fi–only iPads, swipe right-to-left for each step in the route or tap the next step at the edge of the screen (**Figure 9.12**). If you prefer a text list of directions, tap the button at the left of the bar.

At any time, tap the Overview button to see the entire route from the top-down view; on a cellular iPad, first tap once to reveal the toolbar.

3. Tap the End button when you've reached your destination.

Figure 9.12
A trip in progress

> **tip**   When it's time to head home, tap the curved-arrow button (↻)
> between the search fields to swap the starting point and the destination.

> **tip**   You don't need to keep the screen on (burning battery charge) while
> using the turn-by-turn directions. The next steps appear on the lock
> screen as well.

Find Your Friends

My daughter and I recently drove from Seattle to California to visit my
mother, a straight-through trip that took about 15 hours. In the past, I'd
call from the road to update her on our progress, but this time we let
technology provide the updates. My mom installed Apple's free Find My
Friends app on her iPad, which let her see exactly where we were at any
point on the trip. This feature is also helpful when you're with a group of
people at a conference, Disneyland, or other locations where you want to
keep tabs on folks.

Add a friend

Before you can locate a friend, you need his permission to be found. In the Find My Friends app, tap the Add button and choose Add Friends. Enter your friend's email address or name (if he's in your Contacts). He'll receive a request by email or in his Find My Friends app. If he agrees, he'll show up on your map. Tap the Friends button (☰) to view a list of friends (**Figure 9.13**).

Figure 9.13
Found my friend

Find friends temporarily

When your friends are coming together for a limited engagement, set up temporary friendships that expire after a set amount of time.

1. Tap the Add button and choose Temporary Sharing.

2. Add your friends' email addresses to the To field.

3. In the Share Until field, specify when tracking will stop; tap Done.

Be notified when a friend is near (or leaving)

Select a friend and tap the Notify Me button, where you can choose to receive an alert when he or she leaves or arrives at a certain location. You can also set it so your friend is notified when you leave or arrive.

> **tip** If you want to keep using Find My Friends but don't always want to be tracked yourself, tap your location on the map, tap the info button, and then turn on the Hide My Location switch.

10

Be Productive

The iPad isn't Apple's first foray into producing a PDA, or "personal digital assistant." The company created the category—and coined the term, even—with the Newton handheld. But the Newton wasn't adopted as broadly as its upstart competitor the PalmPilot, and when Steve Jobs returned to Apple in 1997, he killed the Newton. As Palm ascended and Windows Mobile devices appeared (and disappeared), people wondered when Apple would get back into the game. I think rumors of a new Apple PDA started floating around the day the Newton died.

A decade later, Apple finally created its modern PDA: the iPhone. Yes, it was a phone, but the phone aspect was just a way to put it into a familiar category. The iPhone, and now the iPad and iPad mini, is capable of storing and making accessible all of your personal information: your schedule, list of contacts, notes, snippets, ideas, and doodles.

Sync Personal Information

Although it's possible to create new events, contacts, and notes on the iPad (detailed in this chapter), most of that information probably already exists on your computer. There are two ways of transferring it to the iPad and keeping it updated: syncing wirelessly using iCloud, Google, Yahoo, or Microsoft Exchange; or through iTunes.

iCloud, Google, or Yahoo wireless sync

The ability to synchronize personal information wirelessly is one of my favorite features of iCloud. If I edit an event on my computer, the change is propagated to my iPad, iPhone, and other computers within a minute or so. If you provided an iCloud account when you set up the iPad, you're already set; it's a great feeling to open your calendar, for example, and just see all of your data there. If not, or if you want to set up another service, do it on the device, not in iTunes.

1. Go to Settings > Mail, Contacts, Calendars and tap Add Account.

2. Tap the button for your provider.

3. Enter your name, email address, and password. Tap Next.

4. Enable the services you want to sync (**Figure 10.1**), and tap the Save button. After a few minutes, your data transfers to the iPad. (These options are also available in the iCloud settings for your primary iCloud account.)

Figure 10.1
Setting up iCloud on the iPad

tip Regardless of your sync method, you may not want every event in the past to appear on your calendar. Go to Settings > Mail, Contacts, Calendars, scroll down to the Calendars section, tap the Sync button, and specify a time period (such as Events 3 Months Back) of events to include during a sync.

Exchange sync

If your company manages its email, contacts, and calendars using Microsoft Exchange, you can tie the iPad into the system with little fuss.

1. Go to Settings > Mail, Contacts, Calendars and tap Add Account.

2. Tap the Microsoft Exchange button.

3. Enter your email address, username, and password. Tap Next.

4. After the information is verified, tap Next again.

5. Enable the services you want to sync (mail, contacts, and calendars), and tap the Save button. After a few minutes, the data transfers.

iTunes sync

iTunes is the gateway between your data and the iPad, whether the data happens to be your music library or your schedule.

note OS X Mavericks no longer supports Sync Services, Apple's technology for syncing this type of data via iTunes, so this option doesn't appear. You'll need to switch to wireless syncing via iCloud or another service.

With the iPad connected, do the following:

1. Select the iPad in iTunes and click the Info button. You'll find categories for contacts, calendars, "other" (notes and bookmarks), and mail accounts. (For details on mail accounts, see Chapter 4.)

2. Click the category checkboxes to enable syncing those items. Under OS X 10.8 Mountain Lion, contacts and calendars are synced with the Contacts and Calendar apps (or, more specifically, with the underlying databases that those applications access). Under Windows, choose the data source from the pop-up menu in the category name; contacts, for example, can sync with Windows Contacts, Google Contacts, or Yahoo Address Book by default.

3. Within each category, choose to sync all items or selected ones.

4. Click the Apply button to make the changes and sync the iPad.

> **tip** It's possible to sync via both iCloud and iTunes. For example, you may want to sync your calendars via iCloud but store only business contacts on the iPad. In that case you'd turn off the Contacts sync option for iCloud and enable specific contact groups in the Info pane in iTunes.

Manage Your Schedule

Some people live and die by their calendars, while others refer to their schedules only occasionally. The Calendar app fits both personalities.

View your calendar

When you open the Calendar app, your schedule appears in one of four views: Day, Week, Month, or Year. Tap a view button at the top of the screen.

Each view has its own focus—the Day view, for example, shows a schedule of the day on the left, with a small red pin indicating the current time. Details about a selected event appear at right (**Figure 10.2**).

Figure 10.2
*Calendar
Day view*

Event
(in list and
in schedule)

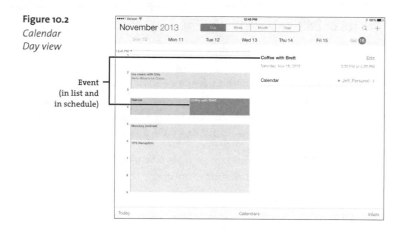

Choose from a variety of ways to switch between dates:

- In the Day view, tap a date at the top of the screen, or swipe left or right on the dates to move in weekly blocks.

- In the Week view, swipe left or right anywhere on the screen.

- In the Month and Year views, scroll up and down.

- Tap the Today button to jump to today's date in any view.

- To view upcoming appointments in a list, tap the Search button (**Figure 10.3**). And, of course, you can type terms to find an event.

Figure 10.3
Sneaky list view

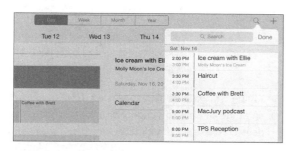

Create or edit an event

A common scenario in my kitchen: While we're making dinner, my wife and I talk about what's happening during the week, specifically events our daughter attends. I often reach for the iPad to view the week, add new events, or edit current ones that have changed. I don't need to go upstairs to my computer to do that. And when I do get to my desk later, the changes are already applied, thanks to wireless syncing.

The following steps illustrate how to create a new event; the steps are almost identical for editing existing events.

1. To create a new event, do one of the following:

   - Tap the + button in the upper-right corner. The Add Event popover appears.

   - Touch and hold at the day or time you want the event to occur. Without lifting your finger, you can drag the event to a specific time.

2. Type a name for the event in the Title field. You can also optionally add a location (**Figure 10.4**).

Figure 10.4
Adding a title and location

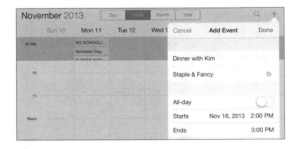

3. Tap the Starts/Ends field and, using the dials below, set a starting date and time and then an ending date and time (**Figure 10.5**). If the event doesn't have a specific time, enable the All-day option. Tap Done.

Figure 10.5
The slot-machine scheduler

4. If the event is recurring, tap the Repeat button and specify how often. Tap Done to return to the previous screen.

5. Tap the Alert button if you want an alarm to go off before the event, and then specify a time. Tap Done.

6. Choose which of your synced calendars the event will appear in. (You can specify a default calendar in Settings > Mail, Contacts, Calendars.)

7. Enter any miscellaneous details in the Notes field.

8. Tap Done.

 If you enter an address in the Location field, the Calendar app makes it a link; tap it to view the location in the Maps app.

To edit an existing event, select it and tap the Edit button (**Figure 10.6**):

Figure 10.6
Editing in Week view

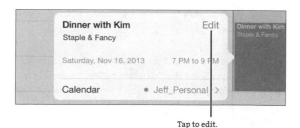

Tap to edit.

You can also grab the top and bottom handles of the event that appear to adjust the start and end times, or you can drag it to a new time.

Reply to an event invitation

When someone invites you to an event using a calendar service that supports the feature (such as Exchange or iCloud), the event appears in the Calendar app as a new invitation.

1. Open the Calendar app and tap the event, which appears with a patterned gray background. You can also tap the Inbox button at the bottom of the screen to view a list of invitations (**Figure 10.7**).

2. Tap Accept, Maybe, or Decline to reply to the invitation.

Figure 10.7
*Incoming
invitation*

You can change your reply later by viewing details about the event and tapping one of the reply buttons.

note If you've entered your Facebook information in Settings > Facebook and enabled the Calendars option, any events made in Facebook show up as invitations. However, you can't respond from the Calendar app; tap the Details button to jump to the Facebook app or Web site.

Hide, show, or edit calendars

In the paper days, to juggle several kinds of events—business, personal, kids' schedules, and so on—you'd need separate physical calendars (or a handful of colored pens). On the iPad, you can include digital calendars for each category, color-code them, and show or hide them as you please.

Tap the Calendars button and tap the ones you wish to hide (the checkmark disappears) (**Figure 10.8**). The events are still there, but they aren't cluttering up your calendar views.

Tap the ⓘ button to change the attributes of a given calendar, like its name and color. Or, tap the Edit button at the top of the Show Calendars popover to create a new calendar. (In the Edit mode you can also change attributes of individual calendars.)

Figure 10.8
Choosing calendars to show

Share iCloud calendars

My wife and I share some calendars so we can better plan for upcoming appointments and also keep track of our daughter's schedule. Here's how you can share your calendar with someone else using iCloud.

1. Tap the Calendars button.

2. Tap the ⓘ button for the calendar you want to share.

3. Under the Shared With heading, tap the Add Person button
   (**Figure 10.9**).

Figure 10.9
Share a calendar.

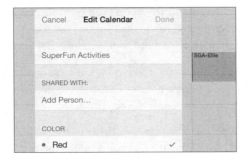

4. Type the iCloud address or contact name of the person(s) you want to
   grant access to the calendar, and then tap the Add button. A notification appears in their Calendar app.

5. If you're on the receiving end, tap the Invitations button and then tap
   Join Calendar.

   tip If you don't want to receive an alert every time an item is changed on
   a shared calendar, go to Settings > Mail, Contacts, Calendars and turn
   off the Shared Calendar Alerts option.

Manage Your Contacts

Over the years, my list of contacts has grown in size to the point where
I know some of the information is out of date, but I don't have the time
or desire to clean it all up. And really, I don't need to. The Contacts app
stores it all for me so I can easily find a person's essential information.

Contacts also ties in to many other areas of the iPad, feeding email addresses to Mail and physical addresses to Maps. When you start typing someone's name in an outgoing email message, you're matching a record in the Contacts app—so you don't have to remember that your cousin Jeremy's address is actually b4conlov3r42lol@aol.com.

Find a contact

The Contacts app presents your contacts in a no-frills address book (**Figure 10.10**). Flick through the list to browse for a contact, or use the vertical strip of letters to advance through the alphabet.

Figure 10.10
*The Contacts
address book*

Drag your finger
down letters to
jump to contacts.

Tap a name to
view its details.

> **tip**   Contacts are listed in order of their last names, but you can change this preference. Go to Settings > Mail, Contacts, Calendars, tap Sort Order in the Contacts section, and change the option to "First, Last." The Display Order option in the same section dictates how each line appears (for example, changing that option to "Last, First" would make my name appear as Carlson Jeff). In either case, the last name appears in bold for easier identification.

If you know the name of the person or company you're trying to find (or even part of the name, or a detail that might be in their information), tap the search field and begin typing. Results appear immediately, with the first one displayed at right (**Figure 10.11**).

Figure 10.11
Find a contact.

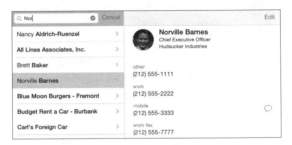

Normally, all contacts are listed, but if you've organized your contacts in groups on your computer, you can display just the contacts from a group.

1. Tap the Groups button at upper left.

2. Visible groups display a checkmark next to them; tap the groups to toggle the checkmark and choose which ones should appear. You can quickly toggle all groups by tapping the All iCloud (or other service) button.

3. Tap Done. The page turns back to the contacts list, showing only those groups' members.

note Although you can view groups on the iPad, the Contacts app offers no way to create new groups or move a person to a new group. You'll need to do that in your desktop software and then sync the changes to the iPad.

Create or edit a contact

I've learned the hard way that I possess a superhuman ability to repel important scraps of paper. Rather than jot down someone's contact information on the edge of an envelope, I prefer to add their details to the Contacts app so I know it won't get lost.

1. Tap the New Contact button (+) to create a new record, or tap the Edit button to change details of an existing record.

2. Tap each relevant field and type the person's contact information.

3. A contact can contain multiple similar items, such as phone numbers. As soon as you start entering information in one field, the Contacts app automatically adds another one below it, anticipating that you may want to add, for instance, a work number and then a home number. To remove any fields already made, tap the red Delete button.

   If you don't see a field you're looking for, such as Job Title, scroll to the bottom of the list, tap Add Field, and choose from the options.

4. For fields with labels (such as Home, Work, or Mobile), tap the current label to view a popover containing alternates. If the one you want isn't listed, choose Add Custom Label and type your own.

5. To add a photo to the contact, tap the Add Photo box, which presents two options:

   - **Take Photo.** The camera interface opens, allowing you to take a picture either of yourself or of someone on the other side of the rear-facing camera. Tap the shutter button to capture the shot, move and scale it to fit, and tap the Use button.

   - **Choose Photo.** Locate and tap an image in your photo albums. Position it in the frame as you'd like it to appear, and then tap the Use button (**Figure 10.12**, on the next page).

6. Tap Done when you're finished creating the contact. You can change details later by tapping the Edit button.

Figure 10.12
Grab an image from your Photos library.

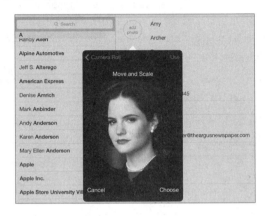

tip If you haven't done so yet, create a record for yourself. Safari uses that information for its AutoFill feature (go to Settings > Mail, Contacts, Calendars > My Info, and specify your entry). It's also good for sharing your details with someone else.

Share a contact

Early handhelds from Palm included an infrared receiver that would let two Palm-wielding people "beam" contact information to each other. Not only was it incredibly geeky, it was extremely useful. In just a few seconds, one person's full contact information was in the other's contacts list. That was before devices were networked; now, if both people are running recent iOS devices (iPhone 5 or later, or fourth-generation iPad or later, including the iPad mini), AirDrop is just like beaming contacts. Or, we can just bounce the same information out to the Internet via text message or into someone's email inbox. To share a record from your Contacts list, do the following:

1. Locate the contact within the list and open it.

2. Scroll down and tap the Share Contact button.

3. If someone is in range of AirDrop, tap their icon. You're done.

   Otherwise, choose whether to send an email or a text message. A new outgoing email or text message appears, containing a vCard file attachment that can be imported into most contact software.

4. Enter the address of the person who will receive the contact.

5. Tap the Send button.

Receive a shared contact

If you're on the receiving end of a shared contact, you can easily add someone's vCard to the Contacts list.

1. If you're using AirDrop, accept the incoming file.

   To receive it in the Mail or Message app, open the message that includes the .vcf file attachment.

2. Tap the attachment to view the contact information (**Figure 10.13**).

3. Tap either the Create New Contact button or the Add to Existing Contact button at the bottom of the information to add the contact.

Figure 10.13
Adding a contact from email

Import Facebook or Twitter contacts

Our important contact information is no longer restricted to our hard drives. Our friends and acquaintances are on Facebook and Twitter, two services where people keep, and frequently update, their personal information. iOS can connect to both services and pull down any data your friends have made publicly available, including bio photos.

1. Go to Settings > Facebook or Settings > Twitter.

2. Tap the Update Contacts button. The iPad temporarily sends a list of your contacts to match them with members' information.

Link contacts

One side effect of having contact information from multiple sources is that you can end up with several entries for one person. To clean things up, you can link contacts to create a unified card—the data is still kept separate, like a personal card and a Facebook card, but they appear as one entry for that person in the Contacts app.

1. Go to a person's card in the Contacts app and tap the Edit button.

2. At the bottom of the screen, tap the Link Contacts button (**Figure 10.14**).

Figure 10.14
Linking similar contacts

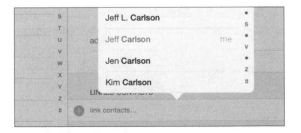

3. In the contacts list that appears, tap the card you wish to link.

4. Tap the Link button.

5. Tap Done to finish. The contact now appears with all of the information, as if it were just one card.

Delete a contact

If you find yourself standing in line somewhere with nothing to do and suddenly feel the urge to purge old records from your Contacts list, do the following:

1. Tap a contact name to view it.

2. Tap the Edit button.

3. Scroll to the bottom of the information and tap the Delete Contact button.

4. In the confirmation dialog that appears, tap Delete Contact. That contact is removed from the list. (Unfortunately, Contacts does not support the near-universal shortcut of swiping across a record to delete it.)

Take Notes

Let's see, the iPad is roughly the size of a pad of paper (or a smaller notepad, in the case of the iPad mini), easy to hold in the hand, and capable of storing a lot of information. When you need to jot down some ideas, the Notes app is ready.

Create a note

Here comes the hard part. Tap the New Note button ( ) and start typing. (Actually, not so hard.)

The first line of the note becomes the title, which appears in the toolbar and in the Notes list. In landscape orientation, that list sits off to the side (**Figure 10.15**); in portrait mode, tap the Notes button to bring up a popover containing all the notes you've stored.

Figure 10.15
The Notes app, viewed wide

Notes list ——

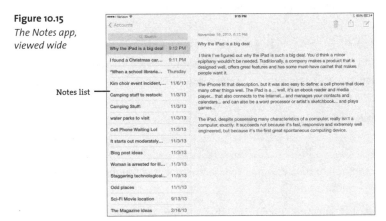

If you're looking for something in particular, enter a term in the search field at the top of the Notes list (**Figure 10.16**).

Figure 10.16
Searching notes, viewed tall

Edit a note

Tap a note in the list to view it. To edit, tap somewhere on the note to place the cursor, and start typing.

Delete a note

There are two ways to delete a note:

- With the note visible, tap the Trash button, then tap the Delete Note button.

- In the Notes list, swipe one finger across a note's title and tap the Delete button that appears.

Sync notes

We've already covered the mechanics of setting up the iPad to sync notes—it's a checkbox in the Info pane in iTunes, or, for wireless sync, a setting under Mail, Contacts, Calendars. But where do the notes go on your computer? On the Mac, they show up in the Notes application. Under Windows, you need Microsoft Outlook 2003, 2007, or later.

Share notes

Tap the Share button at the top of the note to send its contents via AirDrop, send it in an outgoing email or text message, or print it.

tip A lot of alternative note-taking apps for the iPad are available at the App Store. I like PlainText (www.hogbaysoftware.com), which features a clean interface for writing notes and the ability to sync to Dropbox. For more bells and whistles, check out Evernote (www.evernote.com), a catch-all app and Web service that can store text, images, and audio for later. If you prefer writing notes by hand, try Paper (www.fiftythree.com) or other drawing apps, and consider buying a stylus such as the Cosmonaut (www.studioneat.com).

tip If you find yourself doing a lot of typing on the iPad—or if you're taking it along on a trip instead of a laptop—I highly recommend the Apple Wireless Keyboard. Other Bluetooth keyboards also work; although I haven't used them, colleagues rave about keyboards by ZAGG (www.zagg.com), who make Bluetooth keyboards integrated with a case.

Set Up Reminders

Until iOS 5, the iPad, iPhone, and iPod touch didn't offer a to-do list app. It was a curious omission, filled quickly by many developers with apps such as OmniFocus (www.omnigroup.com) and Wunderlist (www.wunderlist.com). Apple finally joined the party with Reminders, a simple to-do app that syncs to iCloud.

To create a new reminder, do the following:

1. In the Reminders app, tap an empty line.

2. Type the title of the reminder and then tap Return on the keyboard.

3. Tap the task name and then the information ⓘ button to edit or add the following details (**Figure 10.17**).

   - Tap Remind Me On a Day to display a notification at a certain date and time.

Figure 10.17
Editing a reminder

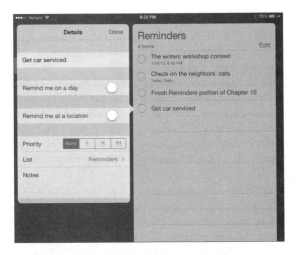

- Tap Remind Me at a Location to trigger the reminder when you arrive at an address or leave it. Search for the location and optionally expand the radius around the spot in the map to set the edge of when the reminder will kick in (**Figure 10.18**).

- Give the task a priority, assign the task to another Reminders list, or add notes in the remaining fields.

4. Tap Done to finish.

Figure 10.18
Editing a reminder

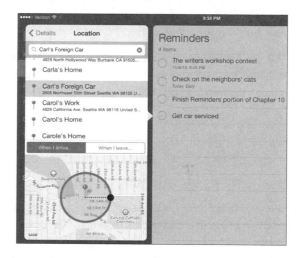

> **tip** Tap the Add List button at the bottom of the screen to create new lists, or tap the Edit button delete existing ones or rearrange the list order. To reorder the reminders themselves, tap the Edit button at the top of the list and then drag the right edge of an item.

> **tip** Reminders are one area where Siri shines. Say "Remind me to take out the trash at 8 p.m. tomorrow" and it will create a new reminder with an alarm all set.

Move Data Files to and from the iPad

The iPad envisions a future where people don't need to worry about file management. Using the Finder under OS X on a Mac, or Windows Explorer on a PC, leads to all sorts of gunk under the hood: *Where are my documents? If the desktop is right there behind my windows, why is it also a folder? Why can't I find the file I just saved?* We've coped with it for years because that was just the way it was. According to Apple's view of the world, an iPad owner shouldn't be exposed to all that. You create something. It's just there. End of story.

But we're not quite there yet. iCloud is a good start, but like it or not, we still have to deal with files, and right now the process of getting them on and off the iPad is a bit of a mess.

There are currently three ways of transferring files that can be opened by applications on the iPad: use a network service such as iCloud, Dropbox, or SugarSync; send them via email; or use iTunes as the gateway.

Sync with iCloud or network services

By far the easiest route to take is iCloud, largely because it's Apple's solution and apps are finally supporting it. New documents in Pages on the iPad, for example, are automatically saved to iCloud. When you open Pages on the Mac, the document is waiting for you. Edit it, and the changes are reflected in iCloud, allowing you to pick up where you left off when you pick up the iPad again.

Another way to transfer files is using an online service such as Dropbox (www.dropbox.com) or SugarSync (www.sugarsync.com). Files stored on the iPad—such as text documents created by the app PlainText—are synchronized with a network server, which you can then access using your computer without needing to plug in a cable. They sync the contents of folders on your computer and make them available on the iPad, where you can preview them or open them in supported apps.

Use email

Because the Mail app recognizes many common file types, you can send an email to yourself, receive the message on the iPad, and view the attachment. See Chapter 4 for more details.

Use AirDrop

iOS 7 includes a new technology called AirDrop that makes it easy to transfer items such as events, contacts, notes, photos, and other items between iOS devices. (It works on the fourth-generation iPad and later, including the iPad mini, and the iPhone 5 and later.)

To set up who can see you using AirDrop, open Control Center and tap the AirDrop button: Contacts Only or Everyone (**Figure 10.19**).

Figure 10.19
AirDrop settings

note   Both iOS and OS X include features called "AirDrop," and although they both work similarly—transferring files to another nearby device—they don't work across platforms. So AirDrop on an iPad will work only with AirDrop on other iOS devices, and AirDrop on OS X will work only with other Macs. Fingers crossed that Apple bridges the gap in the future.

When the AirDrop option is available in a Share pane, tap the icon of the person you want to receive an item (**Figure 10.20**).

Figure 10.20
Sending a photo via AirDrop

Copy to the Apps pane

Apps that can accept outside files appear at the bottom of the Apps pane in iTunes (**Figure 10.21**).

Figure 10.21
Sharing files in iTunes

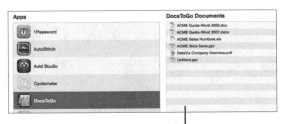

Files on the iPad

1. Click the iPad app that you want to use to open your file.

2. Click the Add button and locate the file you want to transfer. Or, drag the file from the desktop to the Documents pane. The file is transferred immediately; you don't have to sync the iPad.

3. On the iPad, launch the app and use it to open the file.

To get documents back out, reverse the process: Connect to iTunes, and in the Apps pane, select an app, select the file you want, and either drag it to the desktop or click the Save To button and specify a destination.

11

Be Secure

Most of the best qualities of the iPad can also be liabilities. It's portable, so you're more likely to take it with you to a coffee shop or to class, where there's greater chance of losing it or having it stolen. The iPad stores your personal digital information, so a thief would have access to your contact information. Being out "in the wild" also increases the chance that the wireless network you connect to—or even someone at the next table— is scanning for sensitive data like credit card numbers being transmitted.

Security isn't all cloak-and-dagger stuff, though. If you're sharing an iPad among your family, you may not want the kids to get online and down-load all of their favorite albums from the iTunes Store—on your credit card. With some reasonable precautions, you can make your iPad experience more secure.

Set a Passcode to Unlock

The easiest front-line measure you can take to improve the iPad's security is to set a passcode lock that must be entered when the iPad is woken from sleep. The passcode can be a four-digit number or a longer, more secure phrase (**Figure 11.1**).

Figure 11.1
Unlocking the iPad using a phrase

1. Go to Settings > General and tap the Passcode Lock button.

2. To require an alphanumeric passcode, turn the Simple Passcode switch to Off. Otherwise, proceed to the next step to use a four-digit number.

3. Tap the Turn Passcode On button, which brings up the Set Passcode dialog (**Figure 11.2**).

4. Enter a four-digit code, then re-enter it to confirm.

5. The passcode dialog is initially set to appear whenever you wake the iPad. If that's too aggressive, tap the Require Passcode button and choose a timing during which the passcode isn't needed after entering it successfully once.

Figure 11.2
*Setting a
passcode*

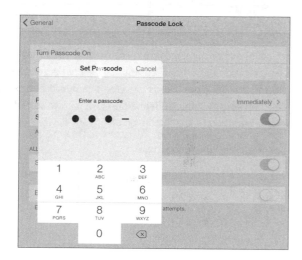

6. To give the passcode lock more teeth, enable the Erase Data option.
   If an incorrect password is attempted ten times, the iPad wipes
   its memory.

note   After you set a passcode lock, you need to enter it whenever you want
to make changes to the passcode settings.

note   Although a Smart Cover will wake the iPad from sleep automatically
when opened, it doesn't bypass the passcode lock. You still need to
enter your code before using the iPad.

iCloud Keychain

As we use iPads more as primary devices (supplementing or even in some cases replacing traditional computers), we're also accessing more Web sites that require passwords and credit card information. In iOS 7 (and OS X Mavericks), Apple added iCloud Keychain to store that information securely and make it available on all of your devices.

To set it up, do the following:

1. Go to Settings > iCloud and tap the Keychain item.

2. Tap the iCloud Keychain switch to turn the feature on.

3. Enter your iCloud password.

4. If this is the first time you're setting up iCloud Keychain, create a four-digit iCloud Security Code. This code is also used in case you need to recover your keychain.

    If you've already set it up on another device, either tap Approve with security code and enter your code, or go to your other device and approve your iPad to use the keychain.

After the iPad is approved, Safari will automatically fill in login forms and give you the option of using stored credit cards when making purchases (see Chapter 4).

tip iCloud Keychain is a welcome feature, but I still prefer 1Password by AgileBits (agilebits.com). Although it's not implemented at the operating system level—a security restriction imposed by Apple—I find its features to be better than iCloud Keychain. That said, I end up using both in different situations.

Use a VPN

When you connect to a public Wi-Fi hotspot, there's a real chance that someone could be analyzing traffic on the network. The way to protect against it (other than to choose not to use public Wi-Fi networks, but that's not a good option) is to set up a virtual private network. A VPN establishes a secure connection to the Internet and protects your traffic from prying eyes.

Your employer may have provided you with VPN connection information, or you might prefer to pay for a service such as WiTopia (www.witopia.net). With the account information, configure the VPN settings so you can switch on the VPN when you need it.

1. Go to Settings > General > Network, and tap the Add VPN Configuration button.

2. Enter the server and settings provided to you (**Figure 11.3**).

3. Tap the Save button.

Figure 11.3
VPN settings

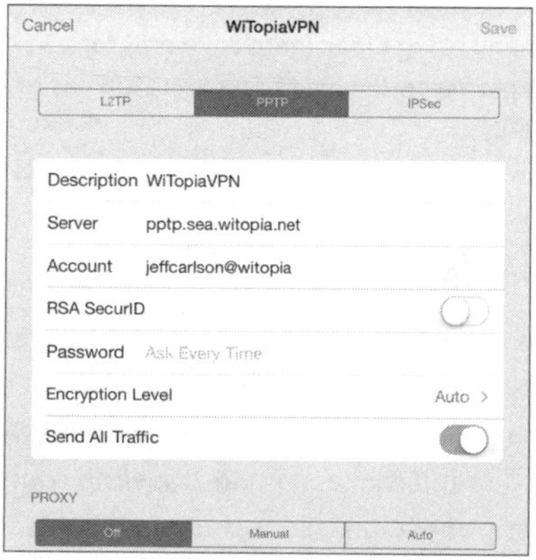

When you want to activate the VPN, return to Settings, where VPN now appears in the main Settings list; tap the VPN switch to On. After the connection is made and authenticated, a VPN icon appears in the status bar (**Figure 11.4**).

Figure 11.4
VPN indicator

VPN active

The VPN settings screen keeps tabs on how long you've been connected; tapping the Status button reveals more information, such as the VPN server name and the IP address assigned to your iPad.

When you no longer need the connection, tap the VPN switch to Off.

> **tip** The VPN connection will close when the iPad goes to sleep, so be sure to reestablish a link the next time you wake it up to maintain secure communications.

> **tip** I recommend using Cloak (getcloak.com) for a VPN, which installs a system profile on the iPad to make setup easier than entering information manually.

Set Up Usage Restrictions

One unsurprising trend I've seen since the iPad was released is that it's a device that gets shared—whether you intend it to be shared or not. A good friend bought an iPad just before leaving on vacation, and he quickly discovered that it makes a great traveling companion. His young son used it on the plane to play educational games and watch videos, and then his wife used it to read ebooks in the evenings. He was lucky to get his hands on the iPad late at night after everyone else went to bed.

The problem is that the iPad isn't set up like a Mac or Windows PC, which have the ability to host multiple separate accounts. So, for example, my friend's email messages were exposed to anyone who wanted to go looking (or accidentally deleting), and he wouldn't have been able to prevent the boy from stumbling onto Web sites inappropriate for a three-year-old.

That's where the iPad's Restrictions settings come in. They don't cover all possibilities—I'd like to see a future version of the operating system have a guest mode optimized for handing the iPad over to someone—but they do help prevent unwanted access.

1. Go to Settings > General > Restrictions to access the settings.

2. Tap the Enable Restrictions button.

3. Enter a Restrictions passcode in the keypad that appears, then enter it again for verification. This passcode is separate from the one you may have set up to lock the iPad.

4. In the first block of settings, determine which apps and services are allowed to run (**Figure 11.5**). When you switch an option to Off, the app disappears from the Home screen. When Location is disabled, the iPad doesn't share its location with apps that request it.

Figure 11.5
App restrictions

5. In the Allowed Content block of settings, choose which media can be viewed (**Figure 11.6**). For example, you may wish to limit videos to movies rated no higher than PG when the kids are awake, and then change the rating or disable restrictions when you want to watch something rated R after the kids have gone to bed.

Figure 11.6
Media restrictions

ALLOWED CONTENT:	
Ratings For	United States >
Music, Podcasts & iTunes U	Clean >
Movies	PG-13 >
TV Shows	All >
Books	All >
Apps	All >

Use Find My iPad

Find My iPad can locate your iPad on a map (even the Wi-Fi–only model, provided it's connected to a hotspot), send sounds or messages to it, or remotely erase its data if you think you'll never see it again.

Set up Find My iPad

Do the following to make sure Find My iPad is active; you don't want to discover too late that you may not have set up the feature.

1. On the iPad, go to Settings > iCloud.

2. Set the Find My iPad option to On.

3. Tap Allow in the dialog that appears to grant the feature access to location data.

note   For Find My iPad to work, the Location Services option (in the Privacy pane) must be turned on.

Take action on a lost iPad

Whether your iPad has fallen behind the back cushion on the couch or fallen into the wrong hands, you can take several actions using Find My iPad to help locate it.

 If you own another iOS device, like an iPhone, download the free Find My iPhone app to locate your devices.

- **Find:** In a Web browser, go to www.icloud.com and sign in. If necessary, click the iCloud link at the upper-left corner of the screen to view the iCloud features, and click the Find My iPhone icon. (Apple uses "Find My iPhone" as a generic name, even if you're not looking for an iPhone.) After a minute or so, your iPad should appear on a map noting its location (**Figure 11.7**).

  Unless there's a solid fix on the iPad's signal, the location may not be accurate.

Figure 11.7
Find My iPad, found

iPad location —

- **Play Sound:** If you suspect you've simply misplaced the iPad in your home (where the top-down map wouldn't provide enough resolution), click the Info button (ⓘ) in the iPad's label or click the iPad in the My Devices list. Then, click the Play Sound button in the window that appears. (The sound resembles a submarine's sonar ping and plays loud, whatever the iPad's volume setting.)

- If you suspect someone else may have the iPad, click the Lost Mode button. You'll be asked to provide a new lock code, optionally enter a phone number, and enter a message (**Figure 11.8**).

Figure 11.8
Find My iPad message being sent and received

Lost iPad

Come back to me little iPad... I have pie!

Call (206) 555-1000

tip I was trying to be cute in the figure above, but if you think someone might have picked up the iPad, you could use the message feature to alert that the iPad is lost, offer a reward for its return, or just include a contact email or phone number.

- **Remote Erase:** In the window of options, click Erase iPad if you think the iPad is gone for good or don't want to risk that someone may get past the passcode and access sensitive information (**Figure 11.9**).

Figure 11.9
Are you sure?

Erase Cayce Air?

All your content and settings will be erased. An erased iPad cannot be located or tracked.

Cancel | Erase

All data on the iPad is automatically hardware-encrypted, so technically, performing a remote erase doesn't actually remove any data; it changes the encryption key, leaving the encrypted data useless. As a result, erasing is fast, taking only a minute and a half.

If the iPad does turn up after a remote erase, connect it to your computer and restore everything from the last backup.

Encrypt iPad Backup

Speaking of the iPad's backup, you could perform remote erasures all day and it won't matter if the computer you sync with was stolen along with the iPad. You can get some measure of relief if you also encrypt the iPad data backup that's stored on the computer's hard disk.

In iTunes with the iPad selected, go to the Summary pane and enable the Encrypt Local Backup option. Backups to iCloud are automatically encrypted.

Control Access to Your Data

To prevent an app from slurping all of your contacts or other sensitive information, iOS requires that you give your permission before an app is granted access to your underlying data. For example, when you first open the Find My Friends app, you're asked if you want to allow it to access your Contacts list. You can control which apps access which data in the Privacy settings.

Go to Settings > Privacy and tap a category, such as Contacts, to see which apps have requested access to its data. You can block access by switching access to Off (**Figure 11.10**).

Figure 11.10

Granting access for apps to use contact data

The Location Services category determines which apps can use the iPad's location. You probably want to grant access to the Find My Friends app (since that's the point of the app), but you may not want Facebook to be able to include your location when you're posting a status update. You can toggle any app's Location Services setting to On or Off.

Limit ad tracking

Here's a sneaky setting that I urge you to change right now. iOS includes a feature called Advertising Identifier, which apps can use to serve targeted ads and collect information about you. To opt out of that service, go to Settings > Privacy > Advertising > Limit Ad Tracking and set the switch to On.

12

Troubleshooting

As I write this, the iPad is not even four years old and in its fifth generation of hardware—quite young by technology standards—and has been joined by the first iPad mini. When something truly new comes out, not just an update to something long familiar, we expect to run into problems that the engineers could not have anticipated under lab conditions.

Yet, the iPad is surprisingly stable. Since receiving my original model on the first day they were available in the U.S., and through all iPad iterations, I've experienced a remarkably small number of crashes and only occasional hard freezes—all of which were easily fixed. (Compare that to an average Mac or Windows PC.)

But that's the point, isn't it? It should all just work, and for most of the iPad experience, it does. When it doesn't, a few simple steps will solve the majority of problems that crop up.

Restart the iPad

I don't want to sound flip, but restarting the iPad is almost a universal cure-all. If the iPad's internal working memory gets full or fragmented, you may see problems or sluggish performance.

1. Press and hold the Sleep/Wake button on the case. A red slider labeled "Slide to power off" appears at the top of the screen.

2. Drag the slider. After a few seconds, the iPad turns off.

3. Count to ten, and then restart the iPad by pressing the Sleep/Wake button until the Apple logo appears.

When an App Crashes

iOS, which runs the show, is designed so that if an app crashes, it does it without affecting other apps or system processes. A crashed app typically just disappears, at which point you'll find yourself back at the Home screen. Tap the app to launch it again and you should be fine.

If the problem persists, check for an update at the App Store. Also read the release notes for the app; developers must submit their apps to Apple for approval, and if a bug has crept in, there's a lag between when an updated version is submitted and when it becomes available.

If that doesn't work, delete the app from the iPad and reinstall it.

If an App Is Sluggish or Unresponsive

Sometimes an app can start to have problems, but not crash outright. In that case, you can force it to quit by doing the following:

1. Press the Home button to go to the Home screen (or switch to another app, as long as the troublemaking app isn't the one running).

2. Double-press the Home button, or swipe up with three or four fingers, to reveal the multitasking interface.

3. Swipe left until the app in question is in the middle of the screen.

4. Flick the app's screen up, as if you're sliding it away from you (**Figure 12.1**). The app quits immediately.

5. Press the Home button to exit the multitasking interface.

Figure 12.1
Force-quitting an app

tip   Every once in a while I see someone quit an app when they exit it normally, perhaps in an effort to free up system resources. They don't need to bother—iOS effectively shuts down apps that aren't running and manages the memory on its own. Occasionally you may run into an app that doesn't properly release its resources, but those instances are rare.

Reinstall an App

If the copy of an app on the iPad has become corrupted for some reason, try a fresh copy. You can do this on the iPad itself or via iTunes.

1. On the iPad, touch and hold the app's icon until all of the icons begin to shake, then tap the Delete button (the X) to remove the app.

2. Open the App Store app on the iPad.

3. Tap the Purchased button at the bottom of the screen.

4. Browse to find the app, or use the search field to locate it.

5. Tap the iCloud download button to install the app (**Figure 12.2**).

Figure 12.2
Reinstall a purchased app.

If it's not convenient to re-download the app from the App Store, sync a new copy from your computer.

1. On the iPad, touch and hold the app's icon until all of the icons begin to shake, then tap the Delete button (the X) to remove the app.

2. Perform a sync (either connected by cable or via Wi-Fi).

3. In the Apps pane within iTunes, locate the app and click the Install button. When you delete an app from the iPad, you still have a backup version in iTunes.

4. Click the Apply button to re-sync and transfer the app back to the iPad.

If that doesn't solve the crashing problem, and it seems clear that other people are not having the same issue, try starting over with the app.

1. Delete the app from the iPad.

2. Also delete the app from iTunes: Choose Apps from the media pop-up menu in the upper-left corner, locate the app in the list, and tap Delete App. Verify that you want to remove the app (**Figure 12.3**), and in the next dialog choose to move the file to the Trash.

Figure 12.3
*Deleting an app
from iTunes*

Are you sure you want to delete the selected app from your iTunes library?

This app will not be deleted from any iOS device that synchronizes with your iTunes library.

☐ Do not ask me again

Cancel   Delete App

tip To find an app in iTunes easily, switch to List view and then click the Kind column heading. Apps are then grouped by device, such as "iPad app" and "iPhone/iPod touch/iPad app." Or, start typing the name of an app in the iTunes search field in the upper-right corner of the window.

3. Go to the iTunes Store and click Download. Since you'd bought it previously, you aren't charged again.

4. Sync the iPad to restore the app.

Connectivity Issues

The iPad was designed to connect to the Internet over a wireless connection, so not having that connection can be frustrating. If you can't connect, try the following:

■ Look for a connection indicator in the upper-left corner of the screen (**Figure 12.4**).

Figure 12.4
Wireless connection icons

Wi-Fi   LTE cellular

The Wi-Fi icon appears when you're connected to a Wi-Fi network. If you're using a Wi-Fi–only iPad, the lack of the Wi-Fi icon means you have no connection. If you're using a cellular iPad, the cellular network is active when Wi-Fi isn't available; you'll see LTE, 4G, or 3G, depending on model and available service.

■ On a cellular iPad, the network indicator icon and signal strength display appear even if you haven't paid for an active data plan. If the signal is there but you can't get online, make sure you've activated a data plan or that you've not reached the limit of your data plan (see Chapter 1 for more information).

■ Try turning off Wi-Fi and turning it back on again. Swipe up from the bottom of the screen to open Control Center and tap the Wi-Fi button. Wait a minute, and then turn it back on.

■ Similarly, try turning off the radio on a cellular iPad and then turning it back on. In Settings > Cellular Data, tap the Cellular Data switch.

■ In the Wi-Fi settings, tap the info (ⓘ) button next to the name of the active network to view its advanced settings (**Figure 12.5**). Then, tap the Renew Lease button, which makes the iPad request a new temporary IP address from the Wi-Fi base station.

Figure 12.5
Renewing the Wi-Fi network lease

Renew Lease button

If the iPad Doesn't Appear in iTunes

If iTunes doesn't recognize the iPad, try these solutions, in order of least to most inconvenient:

- Make sure iTunes is up to date. On the Mac, go to the iTunes menu and choose Check for Updates. Under Windows, choose Check for Updates under the Help menu.

- Connect the iPad to a different USB port on your computer.

- Use a different sync cable.

- Restart the iPad and the computer.

- Download a new copy of iTunes (from www.apple.com/itunes/) and reinstall the software on the computer.

Battery Issues

The iPad's battery requires more power to charge than what many computers put out through their USB ports, which can be a shock to some people who buy the device, plug it into their computers, and see a Not Charging indicator in the status bar. Actually, the iPad *is* charging, but at a very low rate. If you left it asleep and connected overnight, you'd see more power than when you went to bed. See "Charge the iPad battery" in Chapter 1 for more information.

If battery life seems dramatically worse than it did when you bought the iPad, contact Apple about possibly getting a replacement under warranty.

If you're out of warranty and the iPad "requires service due to the battery's diminished ability to hold an electrical charge" (in Apple's words), then you can take advantage of Apple's battery replacement service. For $99, Apple will replace the entire iPad (so be sure you've synchronized it before sending it off). See www.apple.com/support/ipad/service/battery/ for more information.

Reset the iPad

If the iPad does not respond to input at all, it needs to be reset.

Press and hold the Sleep/Wake and Home buttons simultaneously for 10 seconds or until the Apple logo appears. Resetting does not erase the iPad's memory.

Restore the iPad to Factory Defaults

If you continue to have problems, or if you simply want to start over from scratch, you can restore the iPad to its initial state. Remember, this action erases your data from the iPad, so make sure you sync first (if the iPad is working properly) to back up your data.

1. Connect the iPad to your computer.

2. In iTunes, select the iPad in the sidebar and click the Restore button in the Summary pane.

3. In the confirmation dialog that appears, click the Restore button.

   The first time you do this, iTunes downloads a clean version of the iPad's software; subsequent restores pull the data from your hard disk. In either case, you must have an active Internet connection, because iTunes verifies the iPad with Apple's servers.

4. Wait. iTunes copies the data to the iPad, which installs it. After a few minutes, the iPad is ready.

5. In iTunes, choose a backup to restore to the device. Or, you can opt to set it up as a new iPad with just the data that ships on it.

tip For more detailed options, see the following article at Apple's Web site: "iOS: Troubleshooting update and restore issues" (http://support.apple.com/kb/TS1275).

Force the iPad into Recovery Mode

Although it's unlikely, the iPad may get to the point where you can't even select it in iTunes and restore the software. In that case, try forcing the iPad to load in its recovery mode:

1. Make sure that the sync cable is connected to your computer and that iTunes is running.

2. Press and hold the Sleep/Wake button and power off the iPad.

3. Press and hold the Home button.

4. Connect the sync cable to the iPad's dock connector.

The iPad should appear as if it were a new, empty device. Follow the steps in "Restore the iPad to Factory Defaults" to restore the software. For more information, see http://support.apple.com/kb/HT1808.

Index

NUMBERS

1Password
    features, 86
    vs. iCloud Keychain, 234
1x button, tapping, 57
2x button, tapping, 57

SYMBOLS

' (apostrophe), typing, 17–18
! (exclamation point), typing, 16
. (period), ending sentences with, 17

A

A2DP support, using with
    Bluetooth, 46–47
accelerometer, 9
access control, 241–242
ad tracking, limiting, 242
address book, using in
    Contacts app, 217
addresses, copying in Mail app, 102
Adobe InDesign, using with EPUB
    files, 153

Advertising Identifier, disabling, 242
Air Display, 49
AirDrop feature
    in Control Center, 46
    using to share Web pages, 83
    using to transfer files, 229
Airplane mode, 46
AirPlay feature
    in Control Center, 46
    using, 191–192, 194
    using to send photos, 147
AirPrint
    Activator, 50
    compatible printers, 49
    Printer button, 50
    using, 50
albums
    adding photos to, 136–137
    choosing in iTunes, 180
    collapsing, 136
    previewing, 136
    removing photos from, 137
    viewing photos in, 135–136

apostrophe ('), typing, 17–18
app crashes, troubleshooting, 244
app preferences, setting up, 62–63
App Store
    on iPad, 54–56
    in iTunes on computer, 57
Apple Wireless Keyboard, 48, 225
apps
    Buy App button, 56
    Cellular Data settings, 38
    deleting, 247
    exiting, 7
    filling screen with, 57
    finding in iTunes, 247
    force-quitting, 245
    on Home screen, 6
    iCloud button with, 56
    importing from iTunes, 62
    importing photos from, 131
    installing automatically, 57
    launching, 7
    navigating, 8
    organizing into folders, 64–65
    purchasing, 56
    reinstalling, 246–247
    removing in iTunes, 60–61
    removing on iPad, 59–60
    running, 7
    running on iPad, 57
    scaling, 57
    sharing, 61–62
    switching between, 7–9
    transferring, 3–4
    unread, 94
    updating, 58–59
    verifying purchase of, 56
    viewing, 55
    viewing information about, 55
    viewing most recent, 8
Apps pane, copying files to, 230
attachments. *See also* email
    including with mail
        messages, 108
    viewing in Mail app, 100–101
audiobooks
    changing reading speed, 184
    fast-forwarding, 184
    listening to, 184
    rewinding, 184
Auto-Correction feature, using, 20

AutoFill forms in Safari
    enabling, 86
    iCloud Keychain, 88–89
    password management, 87
    storing logins, 87
Automatic Downloads, turning on, 41

B
backing up
    books, 156
    to iCloud, 41
backup, encrypting, 241
Barnes & Noble Nook, 170
battery
    changing, 12–13
    conserving, 13
    indicator, 12
    life, 12
    losing capacity, 13
    power over USB, 12–13
    replenishing charge, 12
battery issues, troubleshooting, 250
Bcc field, 106
Block Cookies privacy setting, 90
Block Pop-ups privacy setting, 90
Bluefire Reader, 170
Bluetooth button, 46
Bluetooth devices
    A2DP support, 46–47
    connecting to, 46–48
    pairing iPad to, 47–48
    removing, 48
Bluetooth keyboards, 48, 225. *See also*
        keyboards; onscreen keyboard;
        split-keyboard
bookmarked pages, opening, 80
bookmarklets, using with Safari, 85
bookmarks
    creating, 80–81
    editing, 81–82
    removing, 82
    returning to in iBooks, 168
    storing, 81
    syncing in iBooks, 168
    using in iBooks, 166
books. *See also* ebooks; EPUB files;
        iBooks app; illustrated books
    advancing to sections, 160
    getting from iBooks Store, 150–152
    landscape orientation, 158

locking rotation, 158
navigating, 159–160
opening, 158
pages left in chapters, 160
reading aloud, 162
reading controls, 159
searching, 163
searching for, 158
table of contents, 160
tapping left margin, 160
turning pages, 159
brightness, adjusting, 11
Brightness slider, 46
browsing history, viewing in
    Safari, 73. *See also* private
    browsing; Safari Web browser
Buy App button, revealing, 56

C

cables, ports for, 46
Calendar app. *See also* iCloud
    calendars
    creating events, 212–214
    Day view, 210–211
    editing events, 212–214
    Month view, 210–211
    navigation bar, 211
    replying to invitations, 214
    views, 210–211
    Week view, 210–211
    Year view, 210–211
calendars
    editing, 215
    hiding, 215
    showing, 215
Calibre, using with EPUB files, 153
camera adapter, using to import
    photos, 129
Camera app. *See also* photos
    capturing images, 117
    capturing video, 119
    composing shots, 117
    exposure, 118
    focus point, 118
    HDR mode, 116
    interface, 117
    modes, 116
    opening, 116
    Square mode, 116
    taking shots, 117

white balance, 118
zooming in on subjects, 118–119
Camera icon, 46
Camera+ app, 116
cameras, importing photos
    from, 128–130
Caps Lock, enabling, 18
Cc field, 106
cellular data network, using, 34–39
cellular service
    activating, 37
    Add International Plan button, 39
    adding, 38
    canceling, 38
    choosing apps for, 38
    DC-HSDPA, 36
    HSPA, 36
    HSPA+, 36
    LTE capability, 36
    measuring usage, 38
    preferences, 37
    View Account option, 38
children, material inappropriate for, 59
Clear Cookies and Data privacy
    setting, 90
Clear History privacy setting, 90
closing Web pages, 76
collections
    deleting titles from, 157
    using with iBooks library, 154–157
comic books, reading, 171
connectivity issues, troubleshooting,
    248–249
contact info, forwarding, 103
contact records, using with locations,
    200
contacts
    adding from email, 221
    adding photos to, 219
    assigning photos to, 146
    creating, 219–220
    deleting, 223
    Display Order option, 217
    editing, 219–220
    fields with labels, 219
    finding, 217–218
    importing from Facebook, 222
    importing from Twitter, 222
    linking, 222–223
    listing, 217

contacts, *continued*
    setting up in FaceTime, 120–121
    sharing, 220–221
Contacts app, address book in, 217
Control Center
    AirDrop feature, 46
    Airplane mode, 46
    AirPlay feature, 46
    Bluetooth button, 46
    Brightness slider, 46
    Camera icon, 46
    Do Not Disturb, 46
    music playback, 46
    Mute button, 46
    revealing, 11
    Timer icon, 46
    using, 46
    volume control, 46
    Wi-Fi, 46
cookies
    blocking, 90
    clearing, 90
Copy option, 22
copying
    files to Apps pane, 230
    images, 23
    photos, 146
    text messages, 113
corrections, making automatically, 20
Cosmonaut stylus, using with
    notes, 225
Cut option, 22

D
data files
    controlling access to, 241–242
    moving, 228–230
DC-HSDPA cellular service, 36
definitions, looking up in iBooks, 169
deleting
    apps, 247
    apps on iPad, 59–60
    bookmarks, 82
    contacts, 223
    items from Reading List, 79
    mail messages, 109–110
    music, 179
    notes, 225
    photos in Photo Stream, 141

    titles from collections, 157
    titles from iBooks library, 155–156
destinations
    searching in Maps app, 202
    swapping with starting
      points, 205
dictation feature, 23–24
directions
    following, 204–205
    getting from Siri, 203–204
    getting in Maps app, 202–203
    turn-by-turn, 205
DMCA (Digital Millennium Copyright
    Act), 191
Do Not Disturb, 44–46
Do Not Track privacy setting, 90
domain name suffixes, entering, 17
downloads, automatic option, 41
drag gesture, 14–15
DRM (digital rights
    management), 152
Dropbox Web site, 228
DVDs
    converting, 191
    DMCA (Digital Millennium
      Copyright Act), 191
Dynamic Type feature, support for, 72

E
ebook readers
    Barnes & Noble Nook, 170
    Bluefire Reader, 170
    comic books, 171
    GoodReader, 171
    Kindle for iPad, 170
    OverDrive Media Console, 170
    from public libraries, 170
    standalone apps, 171
ebooks, importing, 152–153. *See also*
    books; iBooks app
editing
    bookmarks, 81–82
    calendars, 215
    contacts, 219–220
    events in Calendar, 212–214
    notes, 224
    photos, 138
    reminders, 226–227

email. *See also* attachments
    adding contacts from, 221
    using to transfer files, 229
email conversations, reading, 98
email messages, importing photos
        from, 130–131. *See also* Mail
        messages
email spam, dealing with, 111
encrypting iPad backup, 241
EPUB files. *See also* books
    Adobe InDesign, 153
    Calibre, 153
    creating, 153
    downloading, 152–153
    iBooks Author, 153
    Pages, 153
    purchasing, 152–153
    Scrivener, 153
events
    Alert button, 213
    creating in Calendar, 212–214
    editing, 213
    editing in Calendar, 212–214
    recurring, 213
    replying to invitations, 214
    start and end times, 214
    Starts/Ends field, 212
    Title field, 212
Evernote note-taking app, 225
Exchange sync, 209
exclamation point (!), typing, 16
exiting apps, 7
exporting movies, 190
exposure, choosing in Camera
        app, 118
external wireless hard disk,
        buying, 140

F

Facebook, sharing Web pages, 84
Facebook contacts, importing, 222
FaceTime
    account setup, 119
    Change Location button, 121
    setting up contacts, 120–121
    travel setting, 121
FaceTime callers, blocking requests
        from, 124

FaceTime calls
    active call indicator, 123
    audio-only, 122
    Cellular Data settings, 124
    contacts in Favorites list, 124
    making, 122
    Mute button, 123
    recent call log, 123
    setting up exceptions for, 45
    silencing audio, 123
    switching between cameras, 122
    video chat, 122
factory defaults, restoring iPad to, 251
FairPlay digital rights management
        (DRM), 152
file attachments, viewing in
        Mail app, 100–101
files
    copying to Apps pane, 230
    retrieving, 230
    sending via email, 146
    sharing in iTunes, 230
    transferring, 228
Find My Friends app
    adding friends, 206
    features, 205
    Notify Me button, 206
    temporary finds, 206
Find My iPad
    Find action, 239
    Play Sound action, 239
    Remote Erase action, 240
    setting up, 238
    taking action, 239–240
flagging messages in Mail, 104–105
flick gesture, 15
Flickr photo sharing service, 146
Flyover mode
    gestures, 199
    navigating in, 199
    using with maps, 198
focus point, choosing in Camera
        app, 118
folders, organizing apps into, 64–65
fonts, changing in iBooks, 165
force-quitting apps, 245
forms, auto-filling in Safari, 86–89
Fraudulent Website Warning privacy
        setting, 90
friends. *See* Find My Friends app

G

Genius Mixes, playing in iTunes, 183
Genius playlists, creating, 185–186
gestures
    drag, 14–15
    flick, 15
    pinch, 15
    rotate, 15
    shake, 15
    swipe, 15
    tap, 14
    touch and hold, 14
    using two hands, 16
GoodReader, 171
Google wireless sync, 208–210
GPS (Global Positioning Satellite),
    using with maps, 197

H

HandBrake movie converter, 191
hard disk, external wireless, 140
HD movies, playing, 189–190, 194
HDR mode, selecting in
    Camera app, 116
highlight coloring, changing in
    iBooks, 167
highlighted text, returning to
    iBooks, 168
highlighting, removing from
    iBooks, 167
highlighting text
    in iBooks, 166–167
    for selection, 22
Home button, pressing, 4
Home screen images,
    changing, 66–67
Home screens
    adding Web pages to, 82–83
    apps on, 6
    customizing on iPad, 63–65
    going to, 7
    in iTunes, 65–66
    returning to, 8
    switching between, 6–7
Home Sharing feature, using, 192–193
hotspot, using, 39
hotspot indicator, 31
HSPA cellular service, 36
HSPA+ cellular service, 36

I

iBooks app. *See also* books; ebooks
    alternatives, 170
    bookmarks, 166
    creating notes, 167–168
    fonts, 165
    highlight coloring, 167
    highlighting text, 166–167
    installing, 150
    justification settings, 165
    looking up word definitions, 169
    preferences, 160, 165
    returning to bookmarks, 168
    screen brightness, 164
    Scrolling View, 164
    sharing passages, 169
    Sync Bookmarks, 168
    text size, 165
    themes, 164
iBooks Author, using with EPUB
    files, 153
iBooks library. *See also* books
    adding PDFs, 155
    backing up books, 156
    bookshelf, 154
    Collections button, 155
    creating collections, 156
    deleting titles, 155–156
    deleting titles from
        collections, 157
    managing collections, 154–157
    moving titles to collections, 157
    PDF shelf, 155
    rearranging titles, 155–156
    searching for books, 158
    sort options in List view, 154
    switching collection shelves, 155
    titles in collections, 156
    viewing PDF files, 155
iBooks Store
    accessing, 151
    downloading book samples, 151
    FairPlay digital rights
        management (DRM), 152
    locating book genres, 152
    More button, 152
    purchasing books, 151
    re-downloading books, 152
    viewing info about books, 151

iCloud
    backup, 41
    features, 40
    On/Off switches, 40–41
    setting up, 40–41
    syncing data to, 41
    syncing with, 228–229
iCloud account, setting up, 94
iCloud calendars, sharing, 215–216.
        See also Calendar app
iCloud Keychain
    vs. 1Password, 234
    AutoFill contact info, 89
    secure passwords, 88
    setting up, 234
iCloud Photo Stream
    accessing, 140
    adding photos to, 143
    adding subscribers, 143
    comments, 143
    copying photos to albums, 141
    deleting photos, 141
    liking, 143
    Moments view, 142
    Post button, 143
    selecting photos for sharing, 142
    Share button, 142
    sharing, 141–143
    themes, 142
    using, 140–141
iCloud Tabs, using to access
        pages, 74
iCloud wireless sync, 208–210
illustrated books,
        navigating, 160–161.
        See also books
images. See also photos; viewing
        photos
    capturing with Camera app, 117
    changing on Home screen, 66–67
    copying, 23
    gaining USB ports, 129
    saving from Mail, 131
    syncing with folders, 127–128
iMovie app, using, 190
imported photos, syncing to
        computer, 148
imported videos, syncing to
        computer, 148. See also videos

importing
    apps from iTunes, 62
    ebooks, 152–153
    Facebook contacts, 222
    photos from apps, 131
    photos from cameras, 128–130
    photos from email, 130–131
    Twitter contacts, 222
installing
    iBooks app, 150
    updates, 58–59
Internet connection
    personal hotspots, 39
    using cellular data, 35–39
    using Wi-Fi, 30–34
invitations, replying to, 214
iPad
    absence in iTunes, 249
    forcing into recovery mode, 252
    resetting, 250
    restarting, 244
    restoring to factory defaults, 251
    setting up, 3–4
iPad backup, encrypting, 241
iPhone apps, running on iPad, 57
iPhoto app, accessing, 139
iTunes. See also music
    Albums option, 180
    Artists option, 179
    Composers option, 180
    customizing Home screen, 65–66
    downloading, 26
    finding apps in, 247
    Genius Mixes, 183
    Genres option, 180
    importing apps from, 62
    removing apps in, 60–61
    sharing files in, 230
    Smart Playlists, 176–177
    Songs option, 179
    syncing music in, 175
iTunes library, adding PDFs to, 155
iTunes Match
    downloading tracks, 178
    number of songs allowed, 178
    turning on, 177
    upgrading low-quality songs, 179
    using to sync media, 177–179
    yearly cost, 177

iTunes Radio, playing, 182–183
iTunes sync, 209–210

J
JavaScript privacy setting, 90
Junk folder, moving spam to, 111

K
keyboards. *See also* Bluetooth
 keyboards; onscreen keyboard;
 split-keyboard
 Apple Wireless, 225
 switching between, 19
 unsplitting, 18
 using alternates, 19
Kindle for iPad, 170
Kobo app, downloading, 153

L
landscape orientation, 9
Lightning connector, using with
 videos, 194
Limit Ad Tracking, 242
linking contacts, 222–223
links
 bringing tabs forward, 74
 following to Web pages, 71
 viewing URLs for, 74
Location Services, using with
 maps, 197
locations
 Add Bookmark, 201
 copying information, 201
 creating contact records, 200
 Directions buttons, 201
 dropping pins on, 201–202
 finding in Maps app, 196
 getting information
  about, 200–201
 identifying with pins, 199–200
 Report a Problem button, 201
 Share button, 201
locking screen rotation, 10–11
LTE capability, 36

M
M7 motion co-processor, 203
magazines, reading with
 Newsstand, 172

magnification, using to select text, 21
mail
 checking manually, 96
 checking on schedule, 97–98
 getting using Push, 97
 new mail indicators, 98
 Pull to refresh, 96
mail accounts
 navigating, 99
 setting up on iPads, 92–94
 syncing from computer, 92
 troubleshooting configuration, 94
Mail app
 acting on links, 102
 acting on special data, 101–102
 browsing, 95
 Cc field, 95
 copying addresses, 102
 default outgoing account, 106
 enlarging body type, 95
 To field, 95
 From field, 95
 flagging messages, 104–105
 forwarding contact info, 103
 launching Maps app, 101
 outgoing messages, 101
 portrait orientation, 95
 preferences, 106–107
 reading email conversations, 98
 tall view, 95
 viewing file attachments, 100–101
 viewing info about
  recipients, 102–103
 viewing info about
  senders, 102–103
 VIP feature, 103–104
 widescreen view, 94
Mail messages. *See also* email
 messages; Messages app
 active, 94
 adding photos to, 107
 adding videos to, 107
 attachments, 108
 Bcc field, 106
 Cc field, 106
 changing signatures, 107
 copying others on, 106
 creating, 105–107
 dealing with spam, 111

deleting, 109–110
flagged, 94
flagging in Mail app, 104–105
forwarding, 107–108
Mark button, 110
moving, 109–110
moving to Junk folder, 111
replying to, 107–108
searching for, 111
sending, 107
viewing, 94–95
writing, 106
mail recipients, suggesting, 105
mailboxes
    navigating, 99
    previewing mail in, 99
maps
    Compass view, 197
    Current Location button, 197
    GPS (Global Positioning
        Satellite), 197
    Location Services, 197
    navigating, 196
    repositioning, 196
    zooming in and out, 196
Maps app
    changing starting point, 203
    finding locations, 196, 199–202
    Flyover mode, 198
    following directions, 204–205
    getting directions, 202–203
    launching from Mail, 101
    M7 motion co-processor, 203
    recording movement, 203
    Route options, 203
    searching for destinations, 202
    trip in progress, 205
    turn-by-turn directions, 205
    views, 198–199
media, choosing for syncing, 174–177.
    See also syncing media
messages, attaching
        photos to, 145–146
Messages app. See also Mail messages
    sending text messages, 113
    setting up, 112
    using Siri with, 112
MiFi, considering, 34

mirroring video, 48–49
misspelled words, identifying, 23
monitor, extending, 49
motion, reducing, 8–9
movies
    adding manually, 186
    converting DVDs, 191
    exporting, 190
    importing with Photos app, 140
    sources, 190
    sync options, 186
    watching, 187–188
moving
    data files, 228–230
    mail messages, 109–110
multitasking interface, 8
multi-touch gestures
    drag, 14–15
    flick, 15
    pinch, 15
    rotate, 15
    shake, 15
    swipe, 15
    tap, 14
    touch and hold, 14
    using two hands, 16
music. See also iTunes
    deleting, 179
    finding artists, 179
    playing, 179–184
    syncing in iTunes, 175
Music app
    listening to audiobooks, 184
    navigating songs, 181
    Next button, 181
    Now Playing screen, 180–181
    playback controls, 181
    playhead, 181
    Play/Pause button, 181
    Previous button, 181
    Repeat button, 182
    shuffling songs, 182
music playback, 46
music playlists, building, 184–185
Mute button, 46
muting iPad volume, 11

N

navigating
    apps, 8
    books, 159
    in Flyover mode, 199
    illustrated books, 160–161
    mail accounts, 99
    maps, 196
    PDFs, navigating, 161
    photos, 134
    songs in Music app, 181
Netflix app, downloading, 194
network services, syncing
        with, 228–229
Newsstand, reading magazines
        with, 172
Nook ebook reader, 170
notes
    creating, 223–224
    creating in iBooks, 167–168
    deleting, 225
    editing, 224
    printing in iBooks, 168
    returning to in iBooks, 168
    searching, 224
    sharing, 225
    sharing in iBooks, 168
    syncing, 225
    viewing, 224
note-taking apps
    Cosmonaut stylus, 225
    Evernote, 225
    Paper, 225
    PlainText, 225
Notification Center, using, 42–45
notifications
    customizing appearance of, 43–44
    dismissing banners, 44
    Do Not Disturb, 44–45
    FaceTime calls, 45
    Messages, 43
    preferences, 43–44
    reading, 42–43
    Repeated Calls, 45
number keys, accessing, 16

O

On/Off switch
    changing state, 14
    sliding, 14

onscreen keyboard. *See also* Bluetooth
        keyboards; keyboards; split-
        keyboard
    displaying, 17
    hiding, 17
opening
    bookmarked pages, 80
    Web pages, 73
orientation
    changing, 10
    landscape, 9
    portrait, 9
OverDrive Media Console, 170

P

pages. *See* Web pages
Pages app, using with EPUB files, 153
pairing iPad to Bluetooth, 47–48
Paper drawing app, 225
passcode, creating, 4, 6
passcode lock, setting, 232–233
Paste option, 22
PDFs
    navigating, 161
    reading with GoodReader, 171
period (.), ending sentences with, 17
personal hotspots, using, 39
personal information, syncing, 208–210
photo library, transferring, 127
photo management software,
        using, 126–127
photo sharing services, 146
Photo Stream
    accessing, 140
    adding photos to, 143
    adding subscribers, 143
    comments, 143
    copying photos to albums, 141
    deleting photos, 141
    liking, 143
    Moments view, 142
    Post button, 143
    selecting photos for sharing, 142
    Share button, 142
    sharing, 141–143
    themes, 142
    using, 140–141
photos. *See also* Camera app; iCloud
        Photo Stream; images; imported
        photos; Shared Photo Stream;
        slideshows; viewing photos

adding to albums, 136–137
adding to contacts, 219
adding to mail messages, 107
assigning to contacts, 146
attaching to messages, 145–146
capturing, 116–117
copying, 146
editing, 138
grouping and syncing, 127
importing from apps, 131
importing from cameras, 128–130
importing from email, 130–131
navigating quickly, 134
Photo mode, 116
printing, 146
removing from albums, 137
sharing, 145–146
syncing from computer, 126–128
transferring wirelessly, 148
using AirPlay, 147
using as wallpaper, 146
video cables, 147
viewing on projectors, 147
viewing on TV, 147
viewing widescreen, 133
zooming in to, 133
Photos app
    Crop button, 138
    Enhance button, 138
    Filters button, 138
    importing movies, 140
    playing videos, 139–140
    Red-Eye button, 138
    Rotate button, 138
    Save button, 138
    viewing video clips, 139
Photosmith Web site, 148
PhotoSync Web site, 148
pictures. See images; photos
pinch gesture, 15
pins
    removing, 202
    using with map
        locations, 199–202
PlainText note-taking app, 225
Play Sound button, using with Find
    My iPad, 239
playing
    music, 179–184
    songs, 179
    videos, 186–188

playlists. See also Smart Playlists
    building, 184–185
    Genius, 185–186
pop-ups, blocking, 90
portrait orientation, 9
ports for cables, availability of, 46
power button, pressing, 4
powering off, 5
powering on, 3–4
previewing albums, 136
Printer button, finding, 50
printing
    photos, 146
    using AirPrint, 49–50
Printopia, downloading, 50
privacy settings in Safari
    Block Cookies, 90
    Block Pop-ups, 90
    Clear Cookies and Data, 90
    Clear History, 90
    Do Not Track, 90
    Fraudulent Website Warning, 90
    JavaScript, 90
    Smart Search Field, 90
    Website Data, 90
Privacy settings, using, 241–242
private browsing, 89. See also
    browsing history
Project Gutenberg, 152

R
radio, playing in iTunes, 182–183
Reader feature, using, 72
reading
    books aloud with VoiceOver, 162
    email conversations, 98
reading controls, accessing for
    books, 159
Reading List
    deleting items from, 79
    reading pages later with, 79
    Use Cellular Data setting, 79
recovery mode, forcing iPad into, 252
Reduce Motion feature, 8–9
reminders
    creating, 226
    creating lists, 227
    editing, 226–227
Repeated Calls option, 45
Replace option, 22–23

resetting iPad, 250
restarting iPad, 244
Restrictions settings, using, 237–238
rotate gesture, 15
rotating screens, 9

S

Safari privacy settings
  Block Cookies, 90
  Block Pop-ups, 90
  Clear Cookies and Data, 90
  Clear History, 90
  Do Not Track, 90
  Fraudulent Website Warning, 90
  JavaScript, 90
  Smart Search Field, 90
  Website Data, 90
Safari Web browser. *See also* browsing
    history; Web pages
  AutoFill forms, 86–89
  bookmarklets, 85
  changing text size, 72
  creating bookmarks, 80–81
  Dynamic Type feature, 72
  expanding capabilities of, 85
  iCloud Keychain, 88–89
  launching, 70
  opening bookmarked pages, 80
  opening Web pages, 70–71
  private browsing, 89
  Reader feature, 72
  Reading List, 79
  reading Web pages, 70–71
  searching in Web pages, 77–78
  security, 86
  Shared Links, 75
  smart search field, 77
  suggested sites, 70
  viewing browsing history, 73
  viewing URLs for links, 74
  watching videos, 75–76
Safari window
  Back/Next, 71
  bookmarks, 71
  iCloud tabs, 71
  New, 71
  Share, 71
  Smart search field, 71

schedule, managing, 210–216
screen brightness, adjusting, 11
screen orientation, changing, 9–10
screen rotation
  landscape vs. portrait, 9
  locking, 10–11
screens, switching between, 6–7
Scrivener, using with EPUB files, 153
search apps, availability of, 78
searching
  for books, 158
  books, 163
  for mail messages, 111
  text, 162–163
searching Web, smart search
    field, 77–78
searching using Spotlight, 51–52
security
  controlling data access, 241–242
  encrypting iPad backup, 241
  Find My iPad, 238–240
  iCloud Keychain, 234
  passcode lock, 232–233
  Privacy settings, 241–242
  Restrictions settings, 237–238
  usage restrictions, 236–238
  VPN (virtual private
    network), 235–236
selecting
  text, 21
  words, 22
"Sent from my iPad" signature,
    changing, 107
sentences, ending with period, 17
shake gesture, 15
shared contacts, receiving, 221
Shared Links, using in Safari, 75
Shared Photo Stream. *See also* photos
  adding photos to, 143
  adding subscribers, 143
  commenting on, 143
  liking, 143
sharing
  apps, 61–62
  contacts, 220–221
  files in iTunes, 230
  iCloud calendars, 215–216
  notes, 225
  Photo Stream, 141–143

photos, 145–148
Web pages via Facebook, 84
Web pages via Twitter, 84
shortcuts, using, 20
shuffling songs in Music app, 182
side switch, setting behavior of, 10–11
signal strength indicator, 31
SIM card, information stored on, 39
Siri
    accessing, 24
    asking questions, 25
    correcting, 24
    getting directions from, 203–204
    interacting with Messages app, 112
    requesting contacts, 26
    setting up, 4
    using for reminders, 227
    voices, 26
sleep mode, 5
Slide to Unlock control, 4
slideshows. See also photos
    Music button, 144
    playing songs during, 144
    starting, 144
    Transitions button, 144
    viewing, 144–145
Smart Covers
    sleep mode, 5
    waking iPad, 5
Smart Playlists, creating in iTunes,
        176–177. See also playlists
Smart Search Field privacy
        setting, 90
songs
    dragging, 176
    navigating in Music app, 181
    playing, 179
    playing during slideshows, 144
    shuffling in Music app, 182
spam, dealing with, 111
split-keyboard, using, 18–19. See also
    Bluetooth keyboards; keyboards;
    onscreen keyboard
Spotlight, searching using, 51–52
streaming
    media between devices, 191–194
    videos, 190, 194
SugarSync Web site, 228
swipe gesture, 15

sync settings, 176
syncing
    with iCloud, 228–229
    music in iTunes, 175
    with network services, 228–229
    notes, 225
    personal information, 208–210
    photos from computer, 126–128
syncing media. See also media
    selecting items, 174–175
    Smart Playlist, 176–177
    using iTunes Match, 177–179
syncing with computers
    Devices button, 26
    disconnecting iPad, 28
    options, 28–29
    transferring data, 27
    updating system software, 30
    using USB cable, 26
    Wi-Fi sync, 28
system software, updating, 30

T
table of contents, viewing for books,
        160
tabs, bringing forward, 74
tap gesture, 14
television
    connecting to, 147
    playing videos on, 194
text
    auto-correction, 20
    highlighting, 22
    searching, 162–163
    selecting, 21–22
    typing, 16–20
text messages
    copying, 113
    displaying timestamps, 113
    sending, 113
text size
    changing in iBooks, 165
    changing in Safari, 72
thumbnails
    enlarging, 135
    viewing photos as, 134
Timer icon, 46
touch and hold gesture, 14
transferring files, 228–230

troubleshooting
  app crashes, 244
  battery issues, 250
  connectivity issues, 248–249
  forcing recovery mode, 252
  iPad absent in iTunes, 249
  mail accounts, 94
  reinstalling apps, 246–247
  resetting iPad, 250
  restarting iPad, 244
  restoring to factory defaults, 251
  sluggish apps, 244–245
  unresponsive apps, 244–245
TV
  connecting to, 147
  playing videos on, 194
Twitter, sharing Web pages, 84
Twitter contacts, importing, 222
typing
  apostrophe ('), 17–18
  exclamation point (!), 16
  numbers, 16
  text, 16–20

U
updating
  apps, 58–59
  system software, 30
URLs for links, viewing, 74
usage restrictions, setting up, 236–238
USB port, gaining for images, 129
using two hands gesture, 16

V
video, mirroring, 48–49
video cable, using, 147
video chat in FaceTime, 122
video clips, viewing in Photos
    app, 139
video controls
  fill frame, 188
  playback, 188
  subtitles, 188
  volume slider, 188
video files, copying from library, 127
video sync options, 186
videoconferencing. See FaceTime calls
videos. See also imported videos
  adding to mail messages, 107
  buying, 189–190

capturing with Camera app, 119
downloading, 190
dragging, 176
elapsed time, 76
embedded, 75
expand gesture, 76
full screen, 76
playing, 186–188
playing in Photos app, 139–140
playing in Safari, 75–76
playing on television, 194
Play/Pause, 76
remaining time, 76
renting, 189–190
scrubber bar, 76
streaming, 190
streaming services, 194
using Lightning connector, 194
watching in Safari, 75–76
viewing photos. See also images;
    photos
  in albums, 135–136
  Collections view, 132
  disabling controls, 133
  in locations, 134–135
  Moments view, 133–134
  Photo view, 133
  as thumbnails, 134
  Years view, 132
VIP feature, using in
    Mail app, 103–104
Voice Dictation, 23–24
VoiceOver accessibility feature,
    using, 162
volume, muting, 11
volume control, 46
VPN (virtual private network),
    using, 235–236

W
waking iPad, 5
wallpaper
  choosing, 66–67
  using photos as, 146
Web browser. See Safari Web browser
Web pages
  accessing on other devices, 74
  adding to Home screen, 82–83
  canceling, 71
  closing, 76

following links to, 71
jumping to top of, 71
opening, 70–71, 73
reading, 70–71
reading later, 79
reading uncluttered, 72
reloading, 71
searching in, 77–78
sharing addresses via email, 84
sharing via AirDrop, 83
sharing via Facebook, 84
sharing via Twitter, 84
switching between, 74
Web sites
  1Password, 86
  Air Display, 49
  AirPrint Activator, 50
  AirPrint printers, 49
  Dropbox, 228
  EPUB files, 153
  Evernote note-taking app, 225
  Flickr photo sharing service, 146
  GoodReader, 171
  HandBrake movie converter, 191
  Kobo, 153
  note-taking apps, 225
  Pages app, 153
  Paper drawing apps, 225
  Photosmith, 148
  PhotoSync, 148
  PlainText note-taking app, 225
  Printopia, 50
  Project Gutenberg, 152
  SugarSync, 228
Website Data privacy setting, 90
white balance, choosing in
  Camera app, 118

widescreen view, using with
  photos, 133
Wi-Fi
  cellular data network, 34
  in Control Center, 46
  Novatel Wireless MiFi, 34
  turning off, 34
Wi-Fi access point
  Ask to Join Networks, 31–32
  choosing, 31–32
  hotspot indicator, 31
  Lock icon, 31
  signal strength, 31
Wi-Fi network
  connecting manually, 32–33
  disconnecting from, 33
  joining hidden, 33
  lease renewal, 248–249
Wi-Fi sync, setting up, 28
wireless hard disk, buying, 140
Wireless Keyboard, 48, 225
wireless sync
  Google, 208–210
  iCloud, 208–210
  Yahoo, 208–210
word definitions, looking up in
  iBooks, 169
words
  misspelling, 23
  selecting, 22

Y
Yahoo wireless sync, 208–210

Z
zooming in to photos, 133